In the Meantime: Let's Pull the Root! Self-Love Workbook

Learn Self-Awareness, Self-Discovery, and Healing From the Inside Out. Let's Dig Deep! Let's Pull the Root! Let's Break the Cycles!

Lashae Sager

Table of Contents

Introduction

Welcome!

If you are holding this book in your hands, you probably have existential questions. Existential is just a fancy word that means problems that arise from existence itself, those issues and conflicts that come up as part of living in this world. There are many options in this genre, self-help being as diverse a topic as the mind itself. While the human experience varies from human to human, and nobody is going to know all of what you've gone through, there are certain similarities, parallels, and meaningful comparisons we can use to guide one another.

What do you want from this book?

For the purposes of universal symbolism and a handy narrative device, we'll be using the humble plant as an extended metaphor. Because of that wonderful self-similarity we see across all of creation, it won't matter if it's The Mighty Oak or Supple Palm, dandelion, cattail or rose: roots, stems, and leaves are created. A flower, whether a literal fragrant bloom or the "technically a flower but we call it a vegetable" artichoke, is always produced. When the twilight of your years fades tonight, what seeds will you leave behind?

Metaphors break down, of course; you are not photosynthesizing sunlight into energy! Never be one to mistake the map for the actual territory. The lessons and suggested homework will guide you through the process of self-discovery, rediscovery if you think you know yourself, and give you the foundation you need to spring forth with confidence. You hear expressions like 'seize the day' and 'make every moment count,' but what does that actually mean? How does one go from feeling broken and miserable to whole and happy?

Through a series of thought-provoking passages and interactive worksheets, you will dig deep, literally root around in your past and the effects of upbringing on your current state of being. We draw inspiration from the green growing things of this planet as we look at how to dig your roots deep. Past the soil, you are sprouting in and down into the rich, fertile layers tapped by the roots of the tall and strong you wish to be inspired by. Real, lasting change is one of the most difficult undertakings we can attempt, and old habits die hard. Failure can be discouraging, daunting and drives many to quit the journey altogether.

Take heart, stand strong and keep growing. The only time we "lose" the journey of personal development is when we stop proceeding. Give up, stop asking questions and no longer challenge yourself is the death of the spirit, or at least the beginnings of apathy and stagnation. Don't let the waters of your soul run dry or stop moving and putrefy. Stagnation applies to both the human creative spirit and a body of water for the same reason: without fresh input and outflow, one can quickly grow unpleasant. By taking ideas out and examining them, we avoid the backward, regressive mentality that can plague experienced minds and offer those developing these ideas for the first time a solid footing from which to step up out of the known and into the unknown.

This is an interactive book, so be prepared to print out some of these pages or at least have a journal or some blank paper around—no passive absorption of knowledge here. We will be building this up together, watering and fertilizing your roots with tried and true lessons, techniques, and exercises that will leave you feeling healthy, wise, and joyful because self-help is a process, a mindset. There is no Silver Bullet that will forever put to rest those feelings of inadequacy and self-loathing that can spring up on the best of us.

Love is a verb, not a noun; there is no Credits Roll Happily Ever After. Joy takes perseverance, and luck is something you make. This crazy, post-modern world has delivered to us practically everything you can imagine. Yet, so many of us are still plagued with *ennui*, an ill-defined feeling of sadness that creeps in when everything is OK. Chase away the blues by running toward bliss. Learn to embrace love and joy when it feels like you are surrounded by hate and misery. Learn to tell the difference between processing grief and letting it dominate you, and you'll Know Joy instead of having No Joy. Most of all, learn to love yourself and exactly what that means.

We will use some common cliches and proverbs, a few references from pop culture, and some modern fiction to not only keep things relevant with examples you recognize but to show you how to approach myths and parables in general. All too often, a message is lost because we are hanging up on the messenger, missing the point because we followed the wrong thread. If we deconstruct concepts and explore the ideas behind them, we find ourselves enriched for the extra effort.

Did you consider what this book can do for you yet? I want you to state your intention. Make it real. It might be simple or life changing. Whatever you have in mind for your next stage of growth, write it here; if you have a digital format, you can use any blank paper, blank book, or what you have. If you go with loose-leaf pages, get a folder or otherwise keep them together. You may also want to purchase a paper copy of this workbook; that way, you can write in it and take it anywhere.

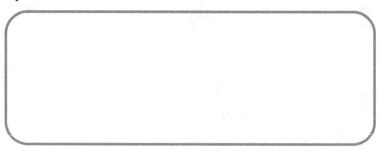

Now, with an objective or two in mind, sit back, relax, and keep that pen handy because the journey of your life is about to begin!

Chapter 1: Root

Root; parents, upbringing, heritage; your inheritance from the past. Do you like where you came from?

They say you can't escape your past, but that's a cliche we can overcome. Personal change is hard because our brain likes to shield us from harm, both real and perceived. Having been wired for survival and little else, our minds will battle against change because it believes what has worked will continue to work. We perceive patterns better than anything else, and changing a pattern that works can throw our minds into revolt. "What works" in the case of brain chemistry is just what has not killed us yet. It is possible to feel a positive change as negative as those minor aches and growing pains steer us away from meaningful growth.

Is the pain I'm feeling a legitimate cue to avoid something or a sign I'm pushing through to the next level? Whether or not our discomfort is growing pains or our body trying to tell us 'no' can be confusing. Learning to tell the difference between "No Pain No Gain" and an actual physical limitation is not hard, but the message can get lost in the noise of daily stress if we let it. That's why it is important to learn how to listen to our bodies. More and more modern science emphasizes the importance of our Microbiome; the collection of bacteria and organisms that live in and on us (mostly in our gut) has more to do with overall health and even our mood and parts of our psychology too.

A "gut feeling" is something we are beginning to understand may actually be a thing! There are neurons down in your stomach lining, only a few hundred but enough to give your belly urges, maybe. Enough, at least, to make a healthy diet even more important than we once thought- and we always knew it was important! They don't remove the appendix unless they have to anymore. It is a kind of storehouse of the good bacteria our guts like and needs. This is all to say that when we begin to address the needs of the mind, body, and spirit, we are looking to clear the mind of chatter, relax the body of tension and let the spirit settle in a better position.

I'm not even going to wax philosophical or spiritual and try to nail down what Soul is beyond this: when I use the terms soul or spirit in this book, I am talking specifically about the thoughts in your head, the feelings in your heart, and the sensations of the body combined; more like how a pep rally at school seeks to raise School Spirit or a cheerleader attempts to instill a spirit of goodwill towards the team. Spirit is invisible, unquantifiable, but undeniable.

With all of this in mind, let's take the first step.

We need to explore our past. There are unconscious motivations lurking around back there, at least, and undiscovered wisdom at best.

Our taproot is the first tiny tendril of input we got from our environment when we were babies, and as we grow, it reminds us of the deepest, strongest root in our foundation. But we were not aware back then. Long-term memory storage doesn't really kick in until age six or seven, meaning our brains *have* memories older than that, but there is no connection to anything. Untethered, these early childhood memories just sort of float around, occasionally getting triggered by smells but for the most part unavailable.

I always found it interesting that this is also how you "delete" information from a computer: you only erase the path to the file you are getting rid of. You are not deleting the data itself. This is how a forensic computer specialist can go in and retrieve files that have been deleted, even years later. It's also why secret-keeping organizations drive a hole through the hard drive when they throw it away: both computers and our brains never really forget anything, merely cut the connections between them. This facet of computer programming was created BEFORE our understanding of how the brain stores information. It is fascinating to think how the brain built another version of itself when we tasked it with making another way to store information. Like, *of course,* that's how we built an artificial memory. That's the only way we know!

Fascinating tangents aside, those super early childhood memories are not available for recall but still actively influencing our thinking. The variety of depth of recall of childhood from person to person is quite wide. Some people seem to have crystal clear childhood memories, while others have only vague recollections, sometimes only feelings or images. Whatever the level of recollection, it can be very helpful knowing what's based on experience and what is not. Before we begin taking an inventory of what makes you *You*, we have to clear some noise from the channel, as it were; the waters are muddy, and we want them clear.

That we might move forward with confidence and in the right direction, let us take a few minutes and think about how we do that.

Think About Thinking

Did you notice I talked about the brain almost as a separate entity? This seeming disconnect between mind and body, the body's very real ability to deceive itself, is paramount to what we need to overcome. Taking unconscious motivations and bringing them into the light of awareness will be required if we are ever to rise above our negative impulses.

There is a train of thought running in the mind of most of us, and even if it's not an actual chattering commentary, the parade of feelings, sensations, and ideas that are flowing through our minds at any given time not only colors our mood but forms our thoughts, as well. Seldom is this train of thought in the present moment, but often dwelling on related things, the past, or daydreams. If this path is through dark places or self-deprecation, think about how you can change the course; nudge it toward positive ideations. We were told as kids, "sticks and stones may break my bones, but words will never hurt me," so much I think many of us forget just how powerful words can be.

I want you to stop beating yourself up. I NEED you to stop filling your head with negative language. No more, *I'm so stupid!* or *Why can't I ever learn?* I have heard this mental habit of negative self-talk rationalized as everything from Irish-Catholic guilt to low-grade depression. Heck, it may have even been true in those cases, but by acknowledging a thing, we can move past a thing. It may take dozens or even hundreds of passes to relearn something that is deeply ingrained in us, but it's OK; we have the rest of our lives to get it right—gentle self-talk, or at least neutral talk when you talk to yourself. Changing your inner dialogue is hard, but oh so worth it. And, again, it might be something you work toward forever, but it gets better and better until the terrible tearing down is less and less frequent, eventually only popping up in moments of weakness or stress.

It is you, talking to you, after all. Be your own support system as much as possible.

What kind of words did your parents use around you growing up? How did they talk to you? Those people that raised you, if not parents, caregivers, and loved ones of every kind, and left indelible impressions on your developing mind. How often is your inner voice *their* voice, your memory recalling their council and not actually you thinking? Consider how young you were, naive, a dry sponge absorbing automatically. Know that human memory is notoriously unreliable. Criminal prosecutors nowadays focus on physical evidence first and eye-witness accounts later. You need to realize how unreliable the details of one's recollections can be and how time affects memory, too.

We polish good memories to a lustrous shine, and negative experiences get replayed in a heated loop, darkening how we feel about them. Post-Traumatic Stress occurs when you get no respite from stress. Living days or weeks on end in Fight Or Flight mode ramps up those parts of the mind-body system and jams them open. Not everyone has the same ability to remember, for that matter. Heck, it may not even be possible to remember that far back at all, but taking time to reflect on your youth and the forces and feelings which surrounded your upbringing can be beneficial. However, you always have to guard against looking backward too much. It is the opposite of self-love when you berate yourself, criticize yourself, and otherwise tear yourself down. Self-hate is a bit extreme, but even small barbs need to be avoided; condition yourself toward using positive, loving self-talk. Make a note of whose voice is degrading you the most- is it your own? Or an influential person from your past you're using the voice of?

Because, yes, the past affects your present and, to a large degree, forms who you are in the future. But now that you've acknowledged this fact, you have power over it. With the power that comes from identifying where you want to change and why, comes the responsibility of doing something about it. The creators of Spiderman like to take credit for the "With Great Power Comes Great Responsibility" quote, but it's from Voltaire, an axiom going back centuries, at least! Since no one actually has superpowers, it speaks of personal empowerment instead; that, yes, mom and dad screwed me up in this way and that way, but now that I know it is screwed up, I can move past it. This isn't to say my parents screwed me up, only that no one has been lucky enough to have been raised by a perfect human being yet, so we all have rough edges that need smoothing off.

As we begin analyzing our thoughts, try to get a sense of what memories associate with what actions; in other words, who are you attaching to what emotions or thoughts from your past? The "Tip of my tongue" thing will happen a lot doing this, so learning to let thoughts and feelings bubble up from the depths of your memory will require the peaceful, still calm center found in the sections below. So keep this little chart handy, both as we go along here and in your day-to-day. Make a note of who you are using in your inner dialogue and weigh against that individual's real-life effect on you.

Influence	Parents	Siblings	Friends	Teachers	Heros, Inspiration	Other
Positive						
Negative						

Too Much?

Maybe you suffer from too much confidence, bordering on arrogance? Do you take the center of every conversation, contradict other's opinions with your own, or one-up every story because you have a better one? Hint: you're not- Stop. At best, this is someone over-excited and too eager to share. At worst, an arrogant, maybe narcissistic blowhard. We all know the type; hopefully, they grow out of it, but some people are just so confident it passes credibility, and they become full of themselves. This is the one tree crowding out the others in our garden metaphor, stealing sunlight with its over-spreading branches and nutrients with its parasitic roots.

This individual can also be the Drama Bomb, a seeming lack of any and all confidence; they throw themselves from task to task, usually from fixer-upper to fixer-upper, always needing moral support and never happy. Stop. If you stop overextending yourself, you will more fully help those you can. Let's take a moment and start asking some really important questions. I have made some statements below; read them and be honest, think about your responses and, if you like, keep the list handy for further exploration. You *should* be answering in the affirmative, with a yes or positive, in all cases!

My feelings matter.

I love myself as much as anyone else.

I am comfortable asking for what I need.

I am comfortable alone.

There are more than one or two things I like about myself.

My self-talk is positive.

I enjoy getting out of my comfort zone.

I don't always have to agree with my friends or family.

I exercise at least a few times a week.

My diet contains as much fresh, healthy foods as possible.

I meet new people and try new things.

I do not feel threatened when someone disagrees with me.

I have dined or gone to a movie alone.

Rooting Around In the Past

How about your parent's parents? Not everyone has the luxury of having living grand and great grandparents, but what you do know can give you insight into the forces that formed your folks and, therefore you. This goes back as many generations as you care to research. The process of investigating one's genealogy can be rewarding, thrilling, even. Depending on the stories, of course, it might be a sobering wake-up call that you're repeating the mistakes of your forebears. It's not always heroes and the upstanding citizens back there but always remember genetics only gives us half the picture, less as far as behavior is concerned. Just like the seeds of an apple will each make different flavored apple trees (flavor variety is maintained by making cuttings, essentially clones), one's offspring may compare in many ways, but one is capable of diverging in so many more.

Any time Nature vs. Nurture gets tested, it seems Nurture wins. While the apple might not fall far from the tree, so much is determined by the environment you grew up in that the rest mostly seems to be genetic health, some unconscious mannerisms, and superficial features. This is liberating; if you were unfortunate enough to be born into an abusive or unhealthy home environment and become aware of this fact, you can change. It may take serious effort and determination, but practice and reflection can unlearn selfish, unproductive behaviors. You can detox a horrible personality with honesty, love, and patience. Said toxic personality has to both admit they have a problem and want to change it, however, just like anything.

While notions of Self-Love are very recent, what kind of self-care, if any, did your parents practice? It looks like going out dancing, arts and crafts, tinkering in the garage (but not escaping into those pastimes), or other activities which stimulate the spirit.

Using family research is an excellent inspiration to use for travel, too. There is only so much you can discover from home. Once you have an ancestor traced back to a specific town, you can often go to their historical records and keep going! My grandma traced one of her roots back to Cork, France, and used that as an excuse to see Paris. While no longer a place, my dad found a side of his family that had come through Acadia, one of the first European settlements in North America. We always knew we were French on both sides, but to have had one of them be from the initial trappers and settlers really resonated with my personal spirit of adventure.

Focusing on the family and your heritage can also give you insight into behaviors and patterns you might not have even observed before. The obvious things like addictions and hobbies are hard to miss, career choices, and even the type of car. Beliefs and habits we pick up from those behind us are hard to mistake, usually. But what about their Way of Thinking? Maybe even unconscious motivations? It can be obvious, too, but overlooked: our "normal" might be miles away from healthy.

Patterns of abuse can persist through multiple generations. All it takes is not socializing with people who are not abusive and isolating the victim so they can't either. This isn't only locking in basements or never letting you leave the house but bad-mouthing friends and actively dissuading you from hanging out with people who don't share the negative behavior, too. Breaking the cycle of codependency or dependency can seem impossible when it's generational or even just severe; people who came from healthy functional lives can still get sucked into abusive relationships. Taking a chance on growth and positive change is always worth it, though, and even failure will at least get you moving in the right direction.

Monkey See Monkey Do

The fallacy of "Do As I Say Not As I Do" should be obvious. As children, we learn by observing first and verbal instruction a distant second. Getting pregnant can be the ultimate inspiration for personal growth. This intuitive understanding that you are about to mold a young life is significant enough to give anyone pause. It would be best if you didn't wait for impending parenting to spook you toward being the best you since change takes time, and you enjoy the benefits now. It would be like waiting until you have a date to brush your teeth- it may be too little too late by the time it's needed the most. That's why it's so important not to grow complacent and take your growth for granted; remember, this is a process, a way of going about things- not a journey with an end.

As long as you keep moving in positive directions, you can't beat yourself up for making errors in judgment. We all make mistakes. The trick is learning from them. In fact, as long as you commit yourself to a lifetime of learning and try, with honest work, to learn from mistakes and attempt to not repeat errors, then you can call them all lessons and avoid getting caught in destructive cycles that stall you at best or are self-destructive at worst. Knowing, learning, and remembering can be tricky, but then again, if personal development were easy, the world would be a different place, indeed!

One of the best tools is to take notes on *yourself!*

Journaling

I kept a journal for much of my teenage years. I actually started one in middle school, but I hated rereading it so much that I hid it from myself and never found it again! A lesson there in self-loathing: I literally hid myself from myself and lost that part. My personality as a teenager was very different than the adult I have become today. Rereading the surviving journals now still makes my skin crawl- I am so unforgiving of myself I'll even try to hold my youthful self to adult standards! It is fun, though, once forgiveness of youthful naivete is granted, the perfect recall that comes from reading your account of something you experienced decades ago. Note-taking really is a terrific memory aid.

It doesn't have to be pages of details. My dad has a weather record he uses to track the daily climate, just a few sentences every day. While its purpose is weather tracking, events and personal reflections inevitably work their way into the entries. Make sure and record the significant events, and the rest is just for you.

Beyond having a detailed record of your own past, journaling has a powerful benefit to your inner psychology. Getting your thoughts out on paper, writing them down, or typing them out gives you a high-resolution image of the thought I don't think is possible without externalizing. You get the same effect when you talk about an idea: getting it out of your head and into the open gives it a dimensionality that is quite simply impossible in the isolation of your thoughts.

There were so many times I remember talking a mile a minute, ideas shooting out of my mouth faster than bullets when I get excited about something when what I'd just said sounded wrong in my own ears, and I'd stop and immediately retract it. Half-baked, I think, is the expression, and truly an idea that has never been breathed can be as doughy and stretchy as an undercooked loaf of bread. Since even our closest loved ones can't always be bothered to act as a sounding board for your every thought, taking it to paper is always a good idea.

Keyboard and computer, blank book and pen, even just loose-leaf pages and pencil, just no dictation: That act of writing, typing, or drawing pulls the thoughts more completely through your head than if you're just talking, so take the extra step and use your hands while recording your impressions. It works so well there is not a college prep or studying guide out there that doesn't recommend taking your own notes. And what is more important than your own life? In fact, once you get used to journaling, it becomes possible to follow your train of thought in real-time. This is a combination of slowing down your thinking and writing fast at first and then just writing faster after a while. You can learn so much about yourself this way; you may want to consider dream journaling.

Dream Journal

If you don't remember your dreams, then these steps can help. If you do, these steps will help you lucid dream. It's simply a matter of telling yourself *I will remember my dreams tonight* as you go to sleep at night. As ever, don't criticize yourself but coax and proclaim; it truly is of no account if you cannot. Dreams are your brain reeling and unspooling. Unguided by conscious desires, dreams are the brain relaxing and drifting. There's no universal language in dreams, few symbols that we all share. Being chased, naked in public, and teeth falling out are typical dream experiences, just as those are also common fears: persecution, vulnerability, and age.

It's just another window into the soul, a glimpse behind the curtain if you will. Dreams shouldn't be anything that motivates you too much; they offer inspiration and an idea about what the brain is preoccupied with. If you work in any kind of creative field at all, hobbies or interests, then tracking dreams will always yield interesting solutions to any design problem.

Even if you don't take the step of recording your experiences, keeping tabs on what is going on in your head-space is crucial. Knowing your own mind is absolutely fundamental to any self-work you may want to do. If you cannot monitor what stimulus in the world affects you the most, you will always be at the mercy of your surroundings. You hear the expression Rise Above a good deal, and this is that: are you going to be buried under layers of reaction and manipulation or push up out of other people's problems and respond by reflecting on the objective factors influencing the situation? That is a roundabout way of saying Don't Be Anyone's Fool. Be extremely wary of people telling you how you should feel about something, setting you up to assume their point of view, and otherwise leading you around by the nose. It can be subtle, so that's why I'm encouraging reflection, at least, and journaling at best.

Dreamboard

A collage, collection of clippings, symbols, and meaningful images of any kind can take the place of books and words if that is more your style. While the benefit of taking the time to write out your thoughts and ideas cannot be overstated, many of us are visual learners or otherwise vastly prefer images to words. Cool, don't worry about it; maybe use a paint marker or other fancy pen to write out keywords in creative ways. Getting the ideas to flow from your hands onto the canvas/posterboard/cardboard is key- express those thoughts into solid reality yourself, as much as possible.

You can share these creations or not. At first, it may feel far too personal, but as you open up and have more and more honest and meaningful conversations, you discover everyone suffers, everyone blisses out, and most people close to you would delight to enjoy your output. Talking to people about your life and your thoughts on life is crucial. Humans, *Homospaiens Sapiens*, only really began to dominate and really take off because we are, at our very core, unrelentingly social. I considered giving you a template, but the shape itself can be fun to experiment with, so use one of the suggestions below or find one you like better.

Humanity and You

Socializing with fellow humans is not typically something we have to remind young people, but something about aging mellows the drive to seek it out and make time with each other. If we haven't made an effort to keep up with the old friends, making new ones can be downright difficult. Factor in the increasingly isolating modern world, and you have a recipe for many people to feel absolutely alone. Getting lost in my own head is something I have had to guard against, anyway, and making time to socialize and get out of the house, even just a little bit, will always be good for perspective, at least.

One grain of wisdom I picked up is to be aware of being surrounded by people who agree with you too much. I mean, in all ways: never disagreeing or even offering differing examples; you may have surrounded yourself with Yes Men, those over-eager to please and accommodate will never help you grow. Balancing between "going with the flow" so much you get swept away and "sticking to your guns" so hard you never change are all part of the challenge, of course. A little give and take is wonderful; all give, or all take is terrible.

Talking about our feelings, fears, and desires is crucial. Emotions were considered a nuisance to be suppressed for so long that when modern psychology was invented in the early 1900s, "talk therapy" was revolutionary. Freud's ideas definitely should be picked through carefully. While most have been discredited, the famous chaise lounge and "tell me about your mother" routine is still used, though nowadays it's more like a chair and general interview. While I believe everyone, the so-called Neural Typical included, can benefit from talking to a psychologist every so often. As long as you have meaningful conversations with people you trust, you might not need to go to a professional. All the same, offering up that brutal honesty when someone really needs it can feel next to impossible. We should be open to the idea of helping, but we usually have to be asked for help- unsolicited advice so often coming off wrong.

Active listening, honest feedback, and a genuine desire to connect are crucial to getting the most out of a conversation. Some people do these things seemingly naturally, those warm, friendly people that radiate welcome and genuinely make you feel appreciated. It can often be a lot of effort, so always be sure to thank people when they go out of their way for you. Please and Thank You should be part of your everyday language anyway, but it can be easy to forget.

Don't just wait for your turn to talk but actually listen, feedback with eye contact, nods, and no interruptions. Even just conveying something related or that you were reminded of can seem like high-roading someone, so be aware of how your words are coming across. Are you sucking all the air out of a conversation? This isn't a lecture: let other people talk. The opposite is true, too: are you silent or passive? Speak up, share! Introversion can become a habit of tight-lipped nods, and some of us never get over being shy. A slight reluctance in a new situation is understandable, but don't if you find yourself afraid to share in your circle of friends!

We love to hear our introverts pipe up, and our shy friends get loose. You will find out *real* quick if they are really your friends or not when you start sharing, too; if you get ignored, interrupted, or contradicted EVERY TIME, then it may be time to move on.

By listening to yourself and listening to others, you can triangulate a path forward. Astute observers will note I gave two metrics and used the word TRIangulation; the third aspect we have to mind as we reach the light is the light itself. What are we striving toward?

Again, suppose we begin conversations about ideas and thoughts, concepts and drives. In that case, we enjoy a richer, more complex relationship instead of based on objects or appearances. Thus "getting deep" doesn't mean you lose touch with the absurd and trivial. Probing the core of something doesn't mean you ignore the surface. We don't want to get so deep we drown, but we want to get out of the kiddie pool, too. Contemplate the cosmos, search for meaning in life but let yourself laugh at farts—one foot in childish wonder, one foot in mature wisdom.

Goals

Every seed has the sun, and beasts are born with instincts or imprint them from their parents. Humans have that *and* the complexities of education and thought. But at the end of the day, year, decade, and lifetime, finding meaning can be a crushing burden for some. For others, the purpose of life is obvious: there is no more need for conscious analysis and deliberation than walking or breathing. Others don't find it nearly as intuitive and find great solace in having a guide of some kind. Priests and spiritual leaders of any kind fall under the social category in my mind- their teachings are the actual goal. Beware the Charismatic Leader, using faith or claim to lure you in but then spinning it their own way.

But don't be so afraid of being led astray you fail to take any guidance. As tempting as it is to believe our story is wholly unique, and while it is to a large degree, the chances are pretty good that someone has been through it, too, or at least shared enough of the main aspects to have a relevant opinion. If you're not drawn to religions, spiritualities, or philosophies, try biographies of people you admire, poetry, or inspirational self-care manuals ;-) Maybe take a few community college classes based on personal interest. Seek out knowledge for its own sake, and you might just discover an unexpected root to follow.

Whatever you choose, the lofty aspiration should motivate you and guide you, not intimidate you and grind you to a halt. The best of us admit when we are wrong, and nobody is right all the time.

Making sense of the bewildering array of choices one can make while setting your intent, balancing the at times conflicted mind, and knowing who's advice to take can be daunting. Yes, journaling, talking with considerate loved ones, and reading or consulting with those whose experience you trust will all enrich the soil in which you grow. But making sure you are level, grounded, and clear-minded will guarantee your personal development is not recursive, self-defeating, or in the wrong direction. Self-love begins and ends with getting in touch with yourself; let's do so now.

Grounding

One of the very first things anyone serious about mental discipline is going to learn is Grounding. In the manic, non-stop world tour that is life, it's packing the bus, tuning your guitars, and balancing the books all rolled into one. If you already know how this works, great. Let's refresh and make sure we are on the same page. If you are not familiar with the term, I guarantee you are familiar with the motions. It even ties into our plant imagery, as I have definitely heard Grounding called Rooting and even Earthing before. It's the effort of letting go and being, being as it is own thing instead of being something; the intentional action of mindful inaction. And it's the only way I know to achieve a state of centered personal attunement consistently. By its very nature, it's a natural stress buster you can use anywhere. Even if you don't ground, these steps will at least help you relax.

It is going to differ from person to person and even from day to day, but grounding is, once you look at brass tacks, simply a way to get to a good default setting—a baseline from which to monitor the rest of your day.

No joke, though. Once you sharpen this skill with a bit of repetition, you will condition it like any action and be able to drop into and out of a calm, clear mindset quickly and easily. The steps outlined below are the method of achieving the desired mental state: once you have done it even a few times, you will be able to mentally switch gears much faster as well as improvise more personalized ways of getting there.

First things first: surroundings. Ideally, the first few times you do this, it is in a quiet, calm place without any distractions or possibilities of interruption. Once learned, though, grounding can be done in almost any surroundings, the noises of the world around you blending into the background as the mind goes silent, the body goes still, and the spirit expands. Once you have found a still place to practice, make sure your clothes aren't binding. Loosen or remove belts, take off shoes and probably socks, and otherwise take stock of any discomfort that might be caused by what you're wearing. You really don't want constrictive clothing in your wardrobe at all, but it is necessary to loosen up, literally and figuratively, when it comes time for grounding.

Usually, music is used to give the mind something to do, but it has to be calm, mellow, even sedate. It can help focus thinking but should be specialized to the task. Meditation music isn't for everyone, and people's irritation with the wrong sounds can be totally jarring and ruin the feeling we are going for. Nature sounds, Ambient, White Noise, and Drone are all search terms you can use to find an audio landscape you like. So is Chant, Orchestral, chimes or bells, and some World; it just has to be nothing that makes you think (no lyrics or complex arrangements) or is too upbeat, high tempo, or overstimulating. While the mental discipline required to ground in silence or a noisy environment is something you can work toward, right now, we just want something to listen to that you don't have to think about but gives the brain something to do when you drift. Ultimately, you can use anything that is unobtrusive, and once grounding has become familiar to you, it might turn out you don't need anything at all.

Visuals? Totally up to the person. Some people like a mandala, candle flame, or holy symbol, but just like the music, it has to be something unobtrusive and neutral, nothing that's going to make your thoughts skitter off. Incense? It can help set the space apart, create the mood, and make it feel special, so sure. Just make sure it's a smell you like, not overpowering, and you've ventilated adequately because most incense is quite strong. Scented oils can work, but you should have one special that is particular to this task so the brain can be triggered specifically. And, again, once you condition your mind toward this mode, a point-of-focus, scent, or music may not even be needed. These objects and stimuli are every bit like Dumbo's magic feather: it's something you hold on to, focus on, that lets the rest of you do its thing but which eventually you should be able to without.

Quiet and comfortable, I want you to sit on the floor, but you can lay down if it's impossible to get comfortable on your bottom. A chair is fine, but the floor is more firm. Popular culture might have you thinking you need to sit in Full Lotus Position, the popular image of the Buddha, legs interlocked and back straight, with chin up and eyes forward is burned indelibly into the popular imagination. OK, fine, you can sit like that if that's comfortable for you, but really we just need you in a place where you can be relaxed, stable, and comfortable. I usually don't lay down only because it's just so darn easy to drift to sleep after the last step that sitting up is preferable- unless you want to use this as a sleep aid! In any case, those of us with limited mobility, surgical or injury-related limits to motion, or just the inflexible shouldn't feel like you have to miss out: just relax. That is key here. Finding a quiet place and comfortable space where no tension is applied to us, we can finally turn inward.

These next steps should be done with your eyes closed or focused on a point in space before you. You can either read through the next bit, memorize it, and then go through the steps after or highlight the sections you want to read aloud and make a recording. Some people *hate* the sound of their voice played back, but this is only because the sound usually

26

resonates through your inner ear and sounds richer when you hear it. In any case, you don't want to try to ground yourself as you read, and hopefully not in front of a glowing screen.

Once comfortable, focus on your breathing for a moment. In and out, you do it thousands of times a day but never have to give it a moment's thought; think about it now. Make sure you're breathing in through your nose and out through your mouth as you get going. This warms the air to body temp before it hits your lungs as well as getting even more oxygen through your lungs, heart, and blood; exhalation is just as releasing of toxins as defecation and urination. It is just that the carbon dioxide we exhale is odorless and colorless. Circular, though, not up/down but round and round.
As we move through these motions, we are working on clearing the mind, not letting ourselves think about the day, the future, or anything, really, beyond breathing and this one present moment. When learning to clear your mind, it is important that you don't chastise yourself, use negative language on yourself or otherwise be mean to yourself when you find your mind drifting. That negative language will only cause perceived harm. The mind will rebel against it and risk this highly beneficial exercise becoming a stressor itself.

All set now, I want you to flex your face a few times. Scrunch your features, wiggle your ears and scalp (or try to), and stretch your jaw, tongue, and eyes; really try to get in touch with everything up there. Face limbered up. I want you to try flexing every muscle on your head at once and hold it AS you slowly inhale. Draw those muscles tight, pull it all in together and hold, tightening the muscle as hard as you can without hurting yourself on the pause. Keep flexing hard until your inhalation is made. Think of a rolling curve on the exhale as you let go of the tension. Let the air ease out through the mouth, not a hard gasp but gentle and smooth.

Now take a few normal breaths, visualize tension releasing using any imagery you like: a knot untying works for me, ice melting into a pool of water, or crumpled piece of paper smoothing out works for others. You might find some other image for integration you find oddly satisfying, so don't be afraid to try new visualizations to see what works best for you.

Next, we move on to the neck and shoulders. Give them a few rolls and rises, feel them move, bones, muscles, and tendons, before breathing in through the nose, flexing and holding, remember the neck flex, holding and then relaxing as we exhale through the mouth. Again, picture the stresses and tensions of the day physically being cast away, dissipating and dissolving, no longer a bother. Take a few normal breaths again before moving on.

Now get the arms flexing, hands, and pectoral muscles; when you go to start the inhalation, it can be rewarding to move the hands and arms in a significant way instead of simply flexing. Pressing your palms together as hard as you can (prayer-like), exaggerating kung-fu moves, or even just power posing like a bodybuilder can all be very empowering. So, again, I ask the reader to play around and find an upper body position that makes you feel great. Inhale, flex and hold, then exhale again; these should be round, connected breaths- the inhale, exhale an unbroken loop.

Abs and lower back are next, so take a second to flex the tummy, tense those little muscles in the lower part of your back and your hips. This is your center of gravity and diaphragm, too: its importance cannot be understated. Sometimes you'll see it called The Solar Plexus, a word in both medical science and spirituality. This area is both a bundle of nerves at the pit of your stomach and the center of your soul, respectively! It's not usually a place we give much thought to about midlife. Then, without a healthy lifestyle, it can be all you think about. Inhale, flex, hold and exhale, letting go of all the tension you can as you do.

Now roll your hips and pucker your butt because it's Root Chakra time! I kid, we're not going to use the Chakra System in this book, but since we're probably sitting down and we are using plant metaphors, I couldn't resist. As we slowly inhale, tense this area and hold it, then let go of the exhalation.

Knees and calves are next. Give them an exploratory flex and release as you breathe normally a few more times. Now do what we have been doing and draw the tension upon the inhale and hold it, flexing as hard as we can, releasing it on the exhale as we let it all go.

Finally, we end with the feet and toes, our roots and root tips if ever there was. Roll your ankles a little and wiggle your toes as you breathe normally a few times. Now inhale, hold and exhale as you flex, tighten and release. The part of you in touch with the earth just got grounded, and now, if you have been using each cycle to release tension, your mind should be clear, and your body relaxed.

It is important to use visualizations and mental discipline to chase troublesome thoughts away. You want to be clear-minded, anyway, but since that's not always possible, you can use positive imagery to at least make sure there is something there for the brain to hold on to as you ease away from the burden.

This is the proverbial Happy Place, and it is very personal. Not that you can't talk about it, just that it varies greatly from person to person. You invent it; it should be calm, relaxing, and a place you have been or seen. That last point is important but can be hard if you have lived a difficult life. It *should* be a place you have been, the mind's way of storing memory, making it so much easier to trigger if it's been there before. Otherwise, a place you have seen will work, too. You simply have to be able to inject yourself into the scene. Strange to tell, my first Happy Place was part of a scene from the climax of an action movie, the main character's chasing and being chased into a rainforest habitat of a zoo. It had a waterfall, lots of plants and, in my imagination, a tame tiger!

Once you get used to achieving this frame of mind, you can get there faster and more easily. One time I grounded myself after gym class in school, and the chatter of people around me turned into an image of my friends playing cards around a table on a rocky outcropping beside the waterfall! None of us played cards at that time. It was kinda funny back then, but it has allowed me to get to my happy place in public places. As far as the people around me are concerned, I'm simply closing my eyes.

Don't underestimate the power of aspirations or a word or phrase to maintain the attitude you want to achieve. It can be as simple as a single word or a few sentences. There are literally entire books of them: powerful, pithy quotes or phrases that you can use to rebalance. I thought to include some, but everyone is going to have a different set of needs in this case, so it is hard to pinpoint anyone that might work. For instance, I am not into wordplay; anagrams and Scrabble are hard for me. But once I saw that "I am Level am I" was a palindrome (a word or phrase that reads the same forward or backward), I liked it as a mantra; it is circular and can be read repeatedly. A mantra is a word for what we've been talking about: a word or phrase you use to clear the mind of other thoughts.

Struggles with self-esteem might see affirmations like "I am worthy" and "I am lovable," while people suffering from racing thoughts or anxiety might go for breathing exercises alone. Depending on your needs, grounding might be little more than a sleep aid, while others will find the practice an indispensable part of starting their day.

Now that we have learned the fine art of clearing the mind, it should be easier to come to terms with life's stressors. It should be fairly straightforward, being able to reflect on the past, grapple with the present, and project an accurate prediction of ourselves into the future. Thus equipped, let's take a personal inventory. Mentally recharged and rebalanced, we think about our roots. Where you come from. Your childhood. Upbringing. Let's make a basic mind map. Reach out and touch the past. Get pen and paper in hand before starting the next section.

Mind Map

Some people just do not think about deep thoughts as a matter of habit. Others may have dug too deep in one place and found themselves in a hole: a narrow thought path with no room to grow. Whatever the case, exploring ideas can be quite literal. Let's start with the word Home. I made the first one for you here. Free-flowing and free association link concepts and ideas you have to the word Home. There are no wrong words. Nothing here will be judged or graded by anyone other than yourself.

Let one thought flow to another- follow tangents as they come. Our minds connect one thought to another, after all, so let's track those links.

Once you have a solid word cloud, column or group, flip the page or go to a clear area and write the word Me or your name. Write in the book, copy them out or use a blank page for any of these or any keywords you care to explore.

- God/Spirituality
- Self
- Family
- Work
- Love

Do the same thing for all the others: fill out as many connected thoughts, feelings, and ideas you have. Let it flow, and don't hold back.

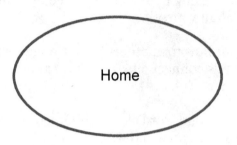

Home

Do this with any core ideas you care to explore your feelings on family, job, love, life, and most importantly, you—the self. Make one with your name in the center and be honest with the free associations- self-love is self-knowledge, and knowing what you think about yourself is crucial. If you already have an ethos (religion, spirituality, etc.), then you can key a map of that. Keep your personal beliefs alive and healthy by challenging them yourself. After all, if you don't explore your own beliefs, turn them around, and inside out, you will be ill-prepared when someone or something challenges those beliefs.

Left unexamined, your ideas about yourself, your family, and your home can grow rigid. If you get too unbending in your ideas, then when (not *if* but WHEN) time changes everything as it inevitably does, you'll find yourself feeling attacked when it comes time to adjust. Even just thinking about them a lot isn't enough; talking or writing it out is the only way to get a final read on topics very dear to us, especially in regards to nurturing a positive self-image.

By examining the elements of the self honestly and dispassionately, we can arrive at the truth. Those parts of ourselves we hate the most we hide the most. Many times when we find ourselves extremely irritated with those closest to us, it is because they are exhibiting behaviors we don't like in ourselves. That one bears repeating, and there's even a cliche that matches it: for every finger you point, there's more pointing back at you (this one works best with a visual aid: if you point your finger at someone, it naturally curves the rest of your fingers back toward yourself!). Having applied this one to me, it turned out to be infuriatingly true: those little things that drive me the most nuts in other people are those things in myself I wish were different.
But wishing never made anything so.

You Can Lead a Horse to Water...

...but you can't make them drink. Change is possible, but it has to come from within- which means the person has to WANT to change. After childhood, we can get pretty set in our ways. Routine becomes a habit, and habit becomes our life. It can be so hard to change major behavior patterns that you might think it's impossible. Even the popular movie Frozen contained a line "People don't really change" in one of its songs, and while that's a fine philosophy to guide you when thinking about others, you owe it to yourself to continue to grow, and that means change. Don't count on others changing; we have to take them at face value. You make your own path, and the people that love you will follow. Not physically, but emotionally. Self-love is taking time and energy to work on yourself; loving you enough to take risks and make long-term projects of personal development. That's not self-indulgent; that's plumb necessary.

I moved to a different state, and nobody followed. However, my family never batted an eyelash when I changed spiritual paths like socks in my teens and early twenties. I was still *me,* and it was that unconditional love and support that helped pull me out of one situation that, eventually, became toxic and cult-like. Had I not had the permission to question authority and think critically about things I desperately wanted to be true, I would have fallen for the lines being fed and stuck around long enough to regret it as much as those that stayed. Had I not had a firm foundation of self-love, respect for myself at least, I would have stayed- just as surely as those that did.

It is the Stand For Something Or Fall For Anything adage in action. By setting out what we know to be true, testing it, and challenging it ourselves, we resist when those beliefs get assaulted by the world around us. With deep roots, even the blows of those we respect most in the world will leave us unmoved on those occasions they turn out to be wrong.

Knowing what to believe doesn't have to be hard. The modern world has suffered the death of expertise in many communities, but you don't have to throw away logic and reason to get to a comfortable mental space. The dangers of comforting yourself with a lie when the truth is difficult are countless; the truth may not always be pretty, but it will always set you free. So before you embrace a change, take on a new habit, or otherwise change your lifestyle, do little digging; don't plant that seed in just any soil, now.

Poor Soil

You have no choice who your parents are. If you're fortunate, both are loving, solid individuals who gave you the tools you need to succeed in life or at least didn't set you up with any major flaws. Chances are, though, that one or two of the negative traits slipped in. Holding a book of self-help and personal change in your hands, it is fully possible they left you with quite a few deficiencies you wish to remedy. You can totally love your parents and still not want to turn into them! This is about where you are drawing your power from and where you want to go.

If they set you up to fail or didn't set you up at all, then the choice is clear: form a new stratum in which to take root or risk growing in ways we don't like if you don't get blown away altogether. As we spread out new branches to catch more light, we can't throw too much shade on where we came from, of course. Did your parents *mean* well? It is certainly possible to do all the wrong things for all the right reasons, but that should never excuse inflicting pain, physical or emotional. Reflecting on our actions helps to ensure we are not repeating the behaviors we were raised with, or if we are, they are positive ones!

It takes motivation, perseverance, and most of all, drive to change a habit. Obvious destructive habits seem easier to change than subtle ones. Coughing up black phlegm gives a smoker pause, but a narcissist or selfish personality only has their slowly dwindling friend base to show them the error of their ways. Give as much as you take; don't always give everything, though; your cup needs a little for you at the end of the day more times than not. It's good to push yourself to exhaustion occasionally, but you shouldn't be redlining every day.

This is where journaling comes into play: we can get so buried in the details of the day that we can miss the forest for the trees. That cliche means being so fixated on the details, on the small things, we lose sight of the big picture. Getting the thoughts and ideas out onto the page allows a more detailed and thorough exploration of the concepts you want to explore.

You can grow up hearing We Are This, or Our People Are That, but you have to understand how much of that is nurture, not nature. No one is inherently anything. Beyond some variable genetics, we are sculpted by our environment and upbringing. In fact, the fairly new field of epigenetics in biology studies how our genes change after conception; our DNA itself mutable to a higher degree than we ever thought. Knowing this, to turn around and say, "So-and-so nation is better, and that group is inferior" quite simply belies your ignorance of the human spirit: nobody is ever truly inferior until they think themselves to be!

Consider a tree growing in the crack of a boulder. First, a sapling wedged in a crevice is weak and frail, barely hanging on, but it eeks out *just* enough nutrients to grow. But grow it does, and pretty soon it has either split that boulder right in two and the cavity filled with a rich soil made from its own leaves and what debris may blow into it its cavity, or it sends roots downward, anchoring the stone further to the ground and becoming bonded to the obstacle that once hindered it, both stronger together. I am talking about thriving in adversity, making the most of your situation, and transforming it or growing out of it if needs be. You are enriching yourself- claiming your space or finding a new place if you can't.

Or, Maybe It's Me

It is one thing to cut toxic people out of our lives, but it is quite another to turn around and challenge what aspects of your behavior may be creating entropy rather than synergy. Are you a force for growth or a force for decay? If we are going to forgive the rest of the world's imperfections, we have to be willing to assume some responsibility for that, too.

Be The Change, I think, is the expression. Some of you give too much, so this is not aimed at all of you.

Personal Inventory

Do you give as much as you take?	Are you actively listening during conversations or just waiting for your turn to talk?	Do you interact with genders differently?	Are your comments mostly complaints, cuts, or critiques?	When was the last time you were wrong and admitted it in?	

This is done for personal reflection and should be kept private; the people you share living space with *should* have no problem respecting personal stuff, and if you fear this sort of personal information might be used against you, then it might be time to reconsider the health of those relationships. If the first thing you can think of to do when you discover someone's journal is to crack it open and start reading, then you might want to check yourself: that's pretty toxic! This is doubly true if you start sharing what you've discovered.

Reaction vs. Response

This is pivotal and could be considered process and growth like chapter 2 or produce and creation in chapter 3. How you interact with people is usually automatic, however, ingrained in you from a young age. So much is done unthinkingly. Unless your social anxiety is higher than the average, you usually don't give too much thought to the details of interpersonal communication after you agonize over it in your teen years. While I would never suggest you go back to hyper-analyzing every word you say, at least give a second thought if you are responding to the details you've just heard or just reacting, acting on past conditioning or knee-jerk replies.

Typically the finer points of how we interact with each other are learned through observation when we are young. The whole "Oh my god, I'm turning into my mother/father!" realization comes out most when we are interacting with each other, language and conversational styles being connected to the same centers of the brain. We can't beat ourselves up over how we talk any more than we can hold our folks responsible for freckles or a unibrow. We can, however, do something about it if we do not like it. Combative, confrontational communication styles can be softened, sarcastic and cynical modes can be neutralized, and any kind of unwanted behavior can be altered.

I have really come to appreciate people who really seem to consider their replies, even taking a moment or two to pause the conversation so they can process. I've seen characters in movies and TV shows get prodded by the speaker, "Hey, what do you think?" while in real life, the person may stare off into space or just look at you, creating a momentary silence. It is typically easy to tell if that stretched silence is apathetic or sympathetic, the engaged listener using nonverbal cues to tell you they are interested: angling the body toward you, prolonged eye contact, social laughter, and nods or widened eyes all let you know you are not boring the person or being bored if you are the listener. The more earnest the revelation, the less a canned or cliched response is acceptable.

Loved ones deserve a well-considered answer. Strangers usually get the superficial. When you accept the possibility that everyone deserves the best of you, those casual questions people use as a greeting, like, "how ya doing?" and "what's up," will give you pause as you consider whether or not the person is genuinely asking about your wellbeing or simply being friendly. It is always funny when someone has something they are in serious need of processing and gets asked How Ya Doing, and then they launch into a whole big thing. If you are around people who care or at least aren't completely self-absorbed, you can expect a little positive feedback. But get into the habit of gushing personal details to people you just meet, and you run the risk of over-sharing or, at most, being considered a Drama Bomb. The term *was* 'drama queen,' but there are just too many men out there wallowing in their emotions to leave it gender-specific. Looking at the sharp distinction between being in touch with your feelings and letting your emotions carry you away is one of the key pieces of a healthy human. Because emotions, thoughts, and actions are so deeply intertwined (explored in-depth below), we cannot fail to appreciate our emotional state, deeply buried or explosively volatile as it may be. There is much made of love, seeking and staying in love, but seldom are we told what that actually means.

Love

How you were loved as a child turns into how you love as an adult. You are unconsciously imprinted to expect and recreate the type of intimate situations you grew up with. Even if you are aware of wanting to change it, you will grow to do unto others as was done unto you without deliberate action and almost constant reflection. *Every time* I see someone struggle to connect, run through a quick series of failed relationships that should at least run their course or otherwise act contrary to how they otherwise do, it can be traced back to upbringing. It got downright trendy to blame your parents for your every fault in the '80s, but even by the '90s and definitely the new millennium, more and more faith is put in the individual to rise above.

Do you know what love is? It can be important to articulate, put it in words so that when the time comes to say 'I Love You,' it is with confidence and honesty. One of the most succinct descriptions of love I have found is when someone else's needs and even wants are as important or more important than your own. With a great deal of shock, teenagers learn the difference between love and lust, and some of us never do. An extreme attraction to someone is not

39

love, but neither is doing everything that person asks of you without question, either. Like everything else, love should be balanced, an equal give and take.

What is Self-Love? I hope to have given you a fair idea about what that means by now and will keep exploring the concept in-depth as we go on but ultimately, it is giving yourself permission to put the self at the same level of importance as those closest to you. When taken to extremes, self-love and self-esteem turn into toxic narcissism and egotism, but when lacking, it leaves you spineless and weak, falling for every con and unable to raise a defense against casual jerks. Yes, with luck, those of you with two little will be able to talk yourselves up and stride forward with confidence, and those of you with a surplus of ego might find the time to share the world with the rest of us.

Ideally, parents pour love on until it overflows, but even parental love can be taken too far, resulting in the proverbial Failure To Launch, an individual smothered with love fails to learn how to be self-reliant. Over-love from parents can lead to a feeling that if others don't give you that same level of devotion, they don't actually love you: nobody loves you the way your parents do (ideally)! Modern economics being what they are, not moving out of the parent's house isn't even the red flag it once was, either. There is something to be said for large extended families all living under the same roof, the "it takes a village to raise a child" adage being very true.

The putting another before yourself aspect of love and loving relationships is seldom perfect. We go through cycles of selfishness and generosity. Some people seem inclined more toward taking or giving, but all things being equal, most people at least *want* to be in the middle, even if many of us can fall into patterns of one or the other. Reflection on your actions and actions of others, aided by journaling for honest, meaningful conversations with people you trust, will help you identify where you land.

Finding love isn't the end all be all in life, either. Sure, finding a partner can give you a great deal of peace and satisfaction, but finding yourself in a committed relationship with someone you are not devoted to can feel just as crushing and isolating as being single, sometimes more so.

...and marriage? Beyond?

Whether or not you want to be married, or even in a long-term relationship at all, should be a personal choice. Many people think they HAVE to. Same with having children: some run through these milestones like they're checking a list, going so fast, only discover once they are married and have kids they want neither! That's why it's so important to take stock of what *you* want and not always do what is expected of you. Yes, we can meet some of the wishes of those you love, but if all it takes for someone to stop loving you is you not doing what they tell you to do, then it's not a love you need. You are no longer expected to sublimate your own happiness for that of your parents, spouse, or society at large. You deserve joy.

I have a few friends who decided not to have kids. From a very early age, they knew it was not something they wanted for themselves. Nearly EVERYONE they confide this to tries to talk them out of it if they don't react like they decided to amputate a perfectly healthy leg. Doctors won't even sterilize them until they are 25, at least, and even then, in one situation, the doctor finally persuaded them to freeze a few eggs in case they changed their mind! Hint: they didn't.

Now, anecdotally (based on personal experience), I have noted that in all these cases, where friends and loved ones decided they didn't want to have kids, they had really difficult upbringings. I don't mean the typical trials and tribulations of growing up or even a little trauma but emotional and physical abuse, poverty, and isolation. Which is all to say, when you meet someone, and they don't have kids and don't seem to miss them, don't assume it's just because they haven't met the right person or hate kids. It's usually personal and seldom any of your business. If you have decided not to propagate more humans into this crazy world, I can't say I blame you.

41

It all comes down to the inner dialogue. What narrative are we telling ourselves? Do we envision ourselves in the future married with children or not? Maybe your image is paired off but not married. Or with a kid but no partner; single parenting is Hard Mode, but if there's one thing this modern world gives us, it's options. What you grew up with is not necessarily what you will get, and as you go forth to strike your own path, it's important to mind your own council.

Respect the Past

Where You Came From is important. If putting distance between those people and you is essential for good mental health, you have every right to do so. I love my family's crest, a coat-of-arms which my dad insists has less to do with our actual pedigree than it does a coincidence of names. Names all come from somewhere, though, and I always liked the imagery and the idea that we are connecting to the past, even if it's distant or marginal.

We are free to draw our own conclusions, and I know at least one of my cousins committed the crest to a tattoo. Even if we're not direct descendants, it reminds him of family. While you have to be careful taking symbols as your own, it's fair game as long as the meaning isn't changed.

It doesn't have to be a crest; it can be anything that reminds us of where we came from. If it's not a situation you care to remember, or you just want to make your own, then you certainly can. Most of the European coat-of-arms are shield-shaped, with a flat or crenelated top and its sides tapering to a point on the bottom; it can be round, square, or any shape you like, I suppose. So the blank I have supplied below should be considered a jumping-off point. Even if you do not intend to make a finished product and hang it up, it is a useful exercise for expressing your feelings about the past, so follow along in any case.

Parents	Childhood
Present	Legacy

As we go through these, it's important not to self-monitor or turn this into a dream board. This should be frank and honest; ideally, it may be something you call back on when you want reassurance, but at worst, it's a badge of honor celebrating what you've overcome. Write, scribble, draw, collage, or hot glue. There's no wrong way to complete this project. Mixed media or neat type, it's yours.

The top left contains words, images, or findings which call to mind your parents: their attitudes, their actions, and life, specifically the strongest associations. You could put older siblings in this category only if they raised you and, by the same token, anyone who had a direct and undeniable impact on your upbringing, next to that, words, images, or findings which force recollections of the environment itself: the place, the other people like siblings, influential friends, and adults. In the lower left-hand side, we have the contemporary zone, for those words, pictures, or things we feel surround our everyday lives: home, family, neighborhood, and friends. Finally, the Legacy Area is a projection of the future we are working toward or even what we want to leave to posterity.

We must honor the past, even if it's a terrible place. I mean honor in the sense of respecting the influence it has upon you and never forgetting where you came from.
We can't help the way we talk: language is developed before we are even aware of it; small children pick up language automatically, absorbing words and meaning almost by instinct. With a little help, they can pick up 2nd and 3rd languages so much faster than adults it can be intimidating. The same is true for so much, however, as we imprint not just words but actions and even thoughts, too. As we develop our own identity, it can be fun to push the boundaries as far as they will go, but most of the time, we spring back to a middle ground of some kind, as comfort in the old and familiar can often take priority over whatever new discoveries had been made.

Hopefully, your background afforded you little to rebel against, though we need not look too hard to find examples of people surviving domestic situations stifling, abusive, or

44

even fatal. In cases when your physical health is in danger, there can be no doubt: run, do not walk, as fast and as far as you can toward safety. There are shelters for abused men as well as women, resources to help anyone escape a situation that's killing them.

As we mature, grow and develop into the people we have always wanted to be, the behaviors and thought paths we learned as children, either indirectly or not, have to be challenged. Going all the way back to No One Is Right All The Time, you have to allow yourself room to grow, and if that means dropping old beliefs which no longer serve you, so be it.

Chapter 2: Stem

The support; what you form from the past, what doesn't bend breaks, raise above.

Where do we go from here? You will want to make your life reflect your dedication to health and wellbeing, both inside and out. You want to grow true- toward an ideal, but you want to be able to bend when forces act contrary to your path. You bend *around* the obstacle. It does not stop your progress. Everyone picks up projects and drops them; you want to carry them forward to completion. You want the wisdom to know when a project is counter to your goals, hurts others, or otherwise needs to be dropped. If your roots run to sand, you possess the ability to redirect and spread out, seeking fulfillment far from where you were born.

I always felt The Unexamined Life Is Not Worth Living was a bit heavy-handed of Socrates until I learned he said those famous words at his trial for teaching an unpopular philosophy where he got the death sentence! As a devout teacher, it makes more sense that he had taken such a hardline stance, but there is a certain amount of power there. Are you going to blindly stumble through life, reacting and being pushed and pulled, or are you going to move forward with certainty and purpose, reaching toward the light?

In education, STEM means Science, Technology, Engineering, and Math, a coincidence this handbook loves. We can apply the observational methodology of science to ourselves, using what works and discarding what doesn't. This doesn't mean dropping traditions or leaving the church unless you discover those things to no longer be useful to you. By looking at the forces and influences of your life the way a technician analyses an experiment, you can drop the useless and self-defeating by focusing on what works.

Ideas and Concepts Not Stuff and Things

This one is a little abstract, literally! It can be hard to put a finger on if it's not something you do already, but once you get it, you'll find yourself able to understand the subtlety and nuances that might have ordinarily been missed. It involves the deconstruction of a thing, looking at the influences and related factors, then putting it back together with greater understanding. At the risk of overthinking, it is looking for What's *Really Goin' On*, the Brass Tacks, the real deal.

When you find yourself talking to people or even thinking to yourself, what is the topic? "Stuff and things" is shoes, car, house, and clothes—hair, jewelry, and all things external that you worry about *for the sake of other people*. Disentangling the pressures of the world and our own desires can be difficult, if not impossible. Being social creatures, we can and should take some cues from society, but that doesn't mean we should bend our entire will to please others. Keeping Up With The Joneses is the major adage associated with this rat race, but it can be smaller scale, too. By analyzing our thoughts on our actions, we can protect against going too far for people who just don't care. How much effort do you put into keeping up appearances? Is the reward there?
If the discussion gets gossipy, casually change tract: *Why* does John drink too much; alcohol in our culture, etc. *What makes* Jane fly off the handle; stress and coping, etc. Be warned; not everyone is going to join you in the deep end. The weather, sports, and 'how ya doing' are generally assumed to be invitations to keep things light. If you are not already the sort of person to bring up motivations, causes, and big ideas like that, it will be an adventure in itself when you start. The people who aren't used to dissecting ideas and exploring concepts might balk or even willfully turn back to the superficial. And that is OK.

Some will consider such musing pointless navel-gazing, but this is the Social aspect we covered above, the benefit of socializing and trading ideas is doubled when the quality of those exchanges is rich. Use the Mind Map to analyze.

Just like anything, however, too much society can be a bad thing. Surrounded by people all the time, always talking, hanging out, and socializing and you will not have any time for reflection. You run the risk of becoming a Follower, toady, or shadow if you find yourself ungrounded. With no identity of your own, you tail those people you respect instead of being inspired by them. This goes back to nobody being right all the time and you not giving of yourself all the time. If you are always chasing this person, but they never contact you first or only when they need something, it's in all ways a one-way street and might be time to reassert your equality.

Cult of Personality is a real thing, and it can be easy to fall into orbit around a strong presence. Charisma is very real, and some people just generate a light you want to be near. This is fine, and knowing what we like and who has the most of it is all part of making friends and finding partners. The danger is when that respect and admiration turn to hero worship. Then the person 'can do no wrong' the possibility exists for abuse. Also, when we think someone is "perfect," the first time we notice anything we don't like, they flip to "flawed."

This is why those passionate, white-hot love affairs that flare up out of nowhere can die just as suddenly: you find that Perfect Person and, placed on a pedestal, they have to make only one slip; they fall as their essential humanity sends you reeling. This is why it's important to guard against absolutes: they are unobtainable. Nobody's Perfect is easy to remember for ourselves, but that means forgiving others, as well.

Aware of the pitfalls of a powerful personality, we can take a moment to address the dangers of seeking wellbeing in commercial America.

Debugging Common Wellness Tips

The term Snake Oil Salesman comes from the people who used to crisscross the country selling bogus tonics and cures in 19th century America. In the modern age, this is At Best someone who's been misinformed and trying to sell you on stuff they think works, and At Worst, someone intentionally trying to separate a credulous believer from their money. The following is all verifiable, backed by science, not feelings. I keep hearing that it is hard to know what to believe, but with a bit of research and knowing what makes a credible source, you can fact-check anything with confidence.

Hydration

Yes, *water is good*. No, you don't need 64 ounces a day, not eight or even six glasses. Much of the water we need comes from dietary moisture, and everyone will metabolize at different rates. There is no magic number; drink when you feel thirsty. Don't ever feel thirsty? Feel for dry mouth, eyes, and cuticle bed; that CAN be atmosphere or environment, but oftentimes if I'm really in a strong flow-state, I won't feel thirsty but will experience those symptoms. The body's need for water to stay properly hydrated cannot be understated but drinking too much water flushes the system too much. Hint: your pee should be pale yellow, not clear!

The first thing I ask myself or my spouse when headaches, tummy aches, and random discomfort come up is: *how was your water today?* It should be almost a joke for how often it gets asked, but more times than not, the answer is *pretty bad, actually*. Because as much as we know it's important, life happens. Things come up, we get distracted, and pretty soon it's noon or even evening, and nary a drop has passed our lips. Don't pay for bottled water- get a filter for the home if city water is bad and a reusable water bottle. There was an entire aisle of insulated water bottles to choose from the last time I went shopping. Find one, carry one. Stay Hydrated, Stay Happy.

Diet

Eat well. Enjoy balanced, small portions throughout the day. What this means to you and what it means to someone else will vary. Too much, as a matter of fact, to dwell too much on. Suffice to say, you NEED greens, fruits, and protein. I'll even go out on a limb and say you need a little sugar and fat, too. Modern diets are heavy in both, of course, so one has to usually lean away from them. You are what you eat in the literal sense of your body turning food into fuel and new cell growth; make sure what you're throwing in the furnace burns clean instead of billows of black smoke. The billows of black smoke in this metaphor are lethargy after meals, not enough energy in general, and eventually ill health.

Listen to the signs of your body; many a self-diagnosis will turn out to be wrong, but many times we can discover things even our doctors do not. That's why it's important to be honest with yourself. Don't ignore your body's pain signals and keep track of them.

Above I stated that most of the time when I feel like garbage, it's because I neglected water? Well, the other times, it's usually food- either terrible choices or nothing. Remember to eat, but make sure you're eating well.

Relationship: Food

1. What kinds of food do you eat?
2. How often do you eat, in what portions?
3. How did your parents eat?
4. What foods did you eat growing up?
5. What changes could be made?

It is easy to take the patterns of our youth with us into adulthood in ways we never consider. We can also use this element for comfort foods and celebrate family, making sure treasured recipes are saved and traditions maintained.

Supplements

I always advise people to talk to their healthcare provider before embarking on a regime on their own, only because strange interactions can affect us randomly. I had someone close to me start getting her friends to take Vitamin D supplements near the onset of the pandemic, as it was supposed to be good for fighting it off covid. However, one of our friend's doctors said with great urgency they should not take extra vitamin D under any circumstances because, in their case, it interacts with a preexisting condition in their lungs, and it would form crystals! They like crystals on their shelf, not lungs, thank you!

A bit of a dramatic example but a reminder to run major changes in diet or lifestyle past healthcare professionals if at all possible.

Fasting, Juicing, and Cleanses

Too much of anything can be dangerous, and these fads don't take into account individual differences, to say nothing of general wellness. While fasting might have its place, eating nothing but juice is bad for gut health, and the only thing that actually cleanses your toxins is your kidneys and liver. If you want to replace one meal with a combo juice, that is usually fine. You can decide to eat one or two simple, spare meals for a few days, great! The modern world has rich diets, and paring it down to truly minimal levels can help get us back in check. Still, the idea that you can get everything you need to live from a single juice or 'detoxify' with a particular regime is unfounded and can be dangerous.

Again, in moderation, sure. Vision quests were undertaken after a fast, but unless you're seeking a waking dream state, you might want to eat something in a day. Ramadan is all about fasting, but you do eat after sundown. You fast before going under anesthesia, so you don't puke all over the doctors, and the human-animal is equipped to Not Die for a few days without food. But unless you have a really good reason, there's just no reason not to eat at all. It's an overcorrection- "oh, I'm not eating right, so I'll just not eat." Some people's positive experiences with juice cleanses are anecdotal, and based on personal experience as they are, it takes it or leaves its territory. But- food and diet are really beyond the scope of this book. To come down too hard on diet stuff beyond the same skepticism you apply to anything would be limited after all. If you want to live off celery juice for a few days, knock yourself out! No, wait, we're listening to body signals, so don't knock yourself out!

The habits and practices we take on should serve us in all ways. If a new hobby or exercise is causing more problems than rewarding us, we owe it to ourselves to listen and take heed. The habit-bound brain might stall and start throwing excuses when we try new things, though, so take care you don't bail before you've given it a chance. If you haven't noticed by now, Balance is important in all things. Too Much of a Good Thing is just as bad as not enough as we can risk overwatering or poisoning the soil with too many nitrates.

They say a new activity will become a habit after 200 repetitions. This is basically a proverb, impossible to prove but gives us a good gauge, some milestones to track progress.

The Still Small Voice

Intuition can be powerful, but it can also be horribly limiting. We need to take stock of what is going on in our unconscious mind if we are going to be able to use it. Once you have grounded yourself and begun keeping track of your inner dialogue (or at least your train of thought), the murky waters of your subliminal motivations become clearer and more apparent. If you are going to tap that boundless creative resource that is the intuitive mind, you are going to want to make sure you are giving your brain the best possible filler. Knowing when it is your inner voice and when it is your parents or voices from the past being repeated is also important to self-love, whether what we're thinking is a response or a reaction. Is this way of thinking actual thinking or your mind replaying memories?

Because intuition isn't some mysterious 3rd party that lobs nuggets of wisdom at you, but the other end of the brain's ceaseless churning. Your active thoughts, the conscious mind you have control over, and hopefully learning even more control is the part you are aware of. Once you ground yourself, get clear-headed with an empty mind, the intuitive voice, the part of your mind you don't typically get access to, gets louder. Those flashes of insight you get, which you are now aware of because you use the open, receptive mindset we've been working on, are not even the end of the road when talking about the intuitive mind. There is so much more to be gained by attempting a more mindful daily attitude.

History is full of engineers, chemists, and inventors who woke up with fully realized solutions to problems in their heads. They were only able to utilize the power of the unconscious mind because they were feeding their brain solid data. Had they been learning incorrect information, their intuitive flashes would not work. We have to be aware of what we are letting ourselves believe. What we allow into our heads affects our decision-making processes and reactions, not just active thoughts; it's essential not to just let yourself believe something because you want to. If it is not true, it is of no service to you.

Dreams are pure intuition; it's a direct line to the emotional heart of your mind-body-spirit connection. Still, some folks just don't remember their dreams, so you shouldn't feel cut off if you don't. You can get to an intuitive solution while awake. You just have to engage the body and distract the brain. How many times have you found an Ah-Ha moment when sweeping or doing some other mundane chore?

If you find yourself stuck and need a creative solution, or just find your mind racing in circles, find a simple task and dive into it. Cleaning is a popular one, yard work and long walks another. When you throw your conscious mind something simple to do, it has to be something you can engage in without thinking too hard about it, and your unconscious mind goes to work on what's *really* bothering you. This can work in the opposite direction. Sometimes you get stomach aches or headaches when you're stressed about something, even if you're not actively thinking about it. Doing what you can to bring the vexing problem to the surface and dealing with it, even just discussing it with someone who cares, is sometimes all it takes.

Whether it is looking to solve a complex problem or vent steam from something you are heated about, learning to settle the stressful body and tap the intuitive mind will only benefit you. A firm hold on your mental bearing will help when those around you are struggling, too.

Empathy & Sympathy

I will draw your attention to an important distinction, even if only for the purposes of this discussion, that of the difference between having empathy for someone and sympathy. When you have empathy for someone, you see their feelings and understand them. A sympathetic reaction is you actually feeling what they are feeling. An empathetic feeling is what you are looking for in day-to-day life, not a sympathetic one; there is usually no such separation between the two in casual conversation, so remember not to confuse our self-discovery tools for conversational English. This is a way of looking at things to not let your emotions carry you away while still being aware of other's feelings.

If your crying makes someone else cry, you can feel responsible for the other's sadness, a burden when you are already unhappy! Some people carry this too far and actively dissuade sympathy, including all human interaction, when they are grieving because the condolences bother them. Well, applied pressure surrounding you has been clinically proven to calm and soothe, so maybe a hug is just what you need. If hugs are not easy to come by, you can buy weighted blankets fairly cheap, the sensation quite a bit like a long, firm hug. The only warning against getting in touch with your feelings is letting your emotions consume you; this being doubly true for the feelings of others.

Sometimes it can't be helped, a tough day or rough exchange happens, and we find ourselves withering or wilting, energies sapped and dragging bottom. No amount of mindfulness and focus will be able to shield you from life's pains. There are a few things you can do to get yourself back on track. Getting shaken up, stressed out, and wound tight is going to happen;

just knowing you can settle down, destress and unwind when you need to can be a boon in and of itself.

Exercise

You need it. You should want it. It can be anything. As long as it raises your pulse, it's good enough for basic wellness. If you want real cardio health, you should break a sweat, but that's not always something we want in a day. Either low-impact walks or activities every day or high-impact, sweaty workouts a few times a week. Just get yourself moving. You are evolution's stupendous, fantastic machine, God/dess's own creation. You were made for survival, constant monitoring for threats, hunting, and gathering. You are now every bit like a big dog in a small apartment. We have to get out and move around, or we'll destroy the furniture. Only instead of chewing, marking, and howling, we end up breaking down. The health risks of a sedentary habit are so well documented I scarcely should have to remind you. Heart health, bone health, mental health- there is not a system of the mind-body-spirit network that isn't affected by you getting active.

Neither of my parents gave me a healthy physical model. Both ate garbage when I was growing up, and neither one exercised regularly. By the time I moved out of the house, however, both had picked up better habits, but it was too late, and I had to develop my own by that time. At first, I had no car, and I still think not owning a car is the way to go if you possibly can, and that had exercise built right in. No, it wasn't until I got a car that I noticed my need for activity. Lower back pain, sore bottom, and general aches and pains, coupled with a general lack of energy and genuine feeling of weakness, made getting up and moving around truly important.

They always say it is easier to Stay in shape than Get in shape, and it is SO true. Losing weight is way harder than just not gaining it in the first place. An ounce of prevention is totally worth a pound of cure, as getting ahead of something is almost always easier than catching up to it. If I have caught you when you are young, great! Start an active hobby now if you haven't already; you've only the rest of your life to reap the rewards. Older, more set in your ways? Well, there are a few things you can do to instill a healthy lifestyle in yourself.

Not active? No problem. Set up a calendar, consider what you plan on doing, and set a goal- one week. If it is a light impact or low effort, go every day: walking the dog, circling the block, a few jumping jacks, and sit-ups. If it's medium or high, you might only engage in the activity once or twice a week. Mix it up: swim and speed-walk, or dance and yoga. Your body will usually tell you when it is ready to go again. When it is strenuous enough to leave you sore, and "feel the burn" is only going to help you push through to the next level before you begin to get burnt out. Again, listen to your body: pain signals aren't always obvious, as distress is communicated through dry mouth, vision problems, and persistent cramping.

DAY	Mon	Tues	Wed	Thurs	Fri	Sat	Sun
Activity							
Time							

Motivation can be challenging. Lists and personal reminders can only go so far—time to tap the positive side of peer pressure and try hooking up with the neighbors. As long as you have even a few, I guarantee someone nearby would like the encouragement and camaraderie that comes with exercising together. Usually, the neighborhood group is limited to everyday activities like walking, running, biking, or yoga. After discussion and getting to know everyone a bit, you might want to try suggesting climbing, swimming, or even Tai Chi or martial arts! Don't be afraid to make unusual suggestions. People are far more open to trying new things with another person. Even if you have no intention of going to something regularly, the experience itself can be its own reward. At the very least, you have met the neighbors and got out of the house. No neighbors, no problem- hit up your friends, co-workers, or acquaintances; everyone knows they need exercise and a little push is usually all it takes.

Barring friends and family, there are apps and programs you can join that will chime, beep or call you to get you going. My uncle had a spiral notebook hanging on a nail with a pencil tied to it by a piece of string next to his door. He called it his Norweigen Personal Trainer (he was Norwegian, so I guess this was OK). He'd time his jogs, the number of push-ups and sit-ups he was doing, and write it all down. That simple object and action kept him on track for decades. Anything you can do to record your activity and inspire not just repetition but growth is good motivation.

Wearable Tech, like Fitbit, can be pretty motivating. Tracking your steps, giving you a pulse reading, and even counting the hours you are asleep is all a great tool to have. Once the domain of early adopters and tech whizzes, my mother-in-law has one now, as does my spouse. Once my spouse got her new one, I inherited theirs. Now we both have those metrics. The friendly reminders it gives me when sitting too long or haven't met my goals have positively influenced me. The fact that it is a machine instead of one of my loved ones means when it catches me at an off moment, I grumble and grouse at the little widget on my wrist instead of an actual human being.

The Nintendo Wii was very interactive, and there are more and more VR systems that require real, frequently strenuous movement. If nothing else, consider a virtual option. In fact, the Wii Fit and Kinect both are defunct, which means they are no longer made and can be found used for far less than they were. New VR systems are definitely more expensive and USUALLY not bought as a health aid! Still, suppose you compare the cost of a Peloton or elliptical. In that case, the few thousand bucks really don't sound that farfetched in the name of fitness.

I have a dog. You quite simply cannot forget to get exercise when you have a furry little friend to remind you. Once out, I met all the other dog-owning neighbors, too. *Boom:* instant social contacts. That is to say nothing of the bonafide medical benefits you get from animal companions, including deeper relaxations, faster healing, and even decreased pain.

Walk, for Many Reasons

At the end of the day, just walk! Fast enough to quicken your pulse, couple it with the Traveling mindset (detailed below), and learn the details of your neighborhood, too. Keep an upbeat demeanor, smile, and nod or go for broke and wave as you say Hello. Learn who your neighbors are and become a familiar sight; this makes neighborhoods safer as everyone begins to recognize one another, and strangers or strange vehicles are more easily identified. Familiarity with one's environment goes a long way toward a feeling of peace and connectedness, too. Just like a dog that walks around the block a few times a day gets exercise AND learns the boundaries of its territory, barking less and generally being calmer, we get that same sense of place. It is a primary human drive to want to do a little recon, stretch the legs and get a feel for the area, too. We were hunter-gatherers for hundreds of thousands of years before the four or five millennia we've been in cities and towns. Take advantage of that instinctual need to wander and go with it.

Fresh air and exercise have so many rewards I can't dwell on it overly much here. It should be obvious by now that even if the health benefits of a bit of exercise don't motivate you, the positive impact on your mind and even the neighborhood should. Sometimes you just can't break away, though. Sometimes even a quick walk is just not in the cards. In those cases, you can do a bit for your body without going anywhere.

Stretch

Quite apart from Exercise, simply stretching is quite essential. It's even automatic, much of the time. Standing up from sitting for too long feels *great*, and we reach upward and arch the back to carry it as far as possible; yoga, calisthenics, Tai Chi, and more dedicate entire disciplines to limbering up and flooding the body with as much oxygen as possible. Pick one, even if it is just the stretches your coach taught you before practice. If you are exercising and not stretching, a*t least* afterward, then you risk cramping and more pain.

Making sure the body is limber is its own reward, and on those days you just can't do any exercise, a few minutes of good stretching will at least give your system a little jostle. Desk jobs especially: set a timer if you need to, but get up and move around for a few minutes every hour; we were simply not designed for long-term inaction.

Mechanically, muscles work by contraction. The Pull and can *only* pull. Stretching those fibers out will not only let more oxygen in but get them back to more of a neutral, relaxed position. Of course, plenty of water will ensure they have the moisture they need to flex, and salt, potassium, and other parts of a balanced diet make sure the electrical impulses pass between brain and body as quickly as possible. So, even right now, Stretch! Stand up, arch that back and reach for the heavens, get up on tiptoe to arch those feet, and breathe deep.

Emotional Intelligence

Do you know what a balance board is? One of those exercise/acrobatic devices which have a cylinder on its side and a flat board set on top? The user stands on the board and balances on the round part. Being keyed into emotions too much can be like that: swaying and pitching this way and that, a steady, level dispositions only possible after much practice.

Being in touch with our emotions is important. If you haven't gotten the memo, 21st Century Humans are allowed to have emotions, express them, and in most cases, respect them. Yes, even men are now expected to be able to say things like "I am happy" or "I am sad." There is a danger, of course, in allowing your feelings too much power. You need to know which way the wind blows, but you can't let it cast you away, either. As we will see below, emotions are one part of a powerful equation, allowing you access to powerful personal development tools.

Think about what we know about emotions: they live in a few glands scattered around the body and the earliest part of our brains to evolve. Just a few specialized centers of your limbic system- your mind-body connection in action. It is the effect of our feelings about the world. Largely uncontrolled, they are a reaction to the world around us, and, in the case of grief and sadness, we are expected to let them run their course. However, you can get in the middle of the emotional-mental process, and stopping the tears before they come can be a handy trick to know. Such interventions are not recommended—those upswells of feeling are all a part of the whole body's processes. Just like the balance board sways back and forth, "pulling it together" long enough to get through the day should be followed by a period of unabashed weeping or at least open grieving. By not processing your feelings, you run the risk of bottling those negative feelings up and having them turn toxic.

Some people seem to revel in misery, nursing a wound long after most folks will have moved on. It is never our place to say how one should feel, but there's a point where a friend or loved one can step in and offer to break the cycle. Suppose we have a big family or large social circle. In that case, we'll have a diverse assortment of contacts to nudge us in the right direction when we run astray. The people we choose to surround ourselves with, more and more a conscious choice the older we get, should never be left to twist in the wind but be aided and supported every chance we get.

Branch Out

It can be tempting to surround yourself exclusively with people who agree with you, and for the most part, that will happen naturally. There's nothing wrong with consensus, of course, but part of growing as a human is understanding the points of view of others. Not cutting people out of our lives for differing opinions, forgiving minor and even the occasional medium trespass is what is required to maintain a long-term relationship of any kind. Have the strength and courage to cut people out of your life for major abuses and take the time and wisdom to determine if you should ever let them back in. Realize what really matters is actions first, and words second; thoughts a distant third. Likes and dislikes become superficial traits beyond a certain point.

When seeking a mate, we often set Deal Breakers for ourselves, and this kind of filtering mentality can persist when we're adding to our circle of friends. If you only have a few criteria on this, that's fine. As mentioned above, it is important to know what we stand for, and choosing friends who share a few core values is crucial. However, it needs to be tempered with the knowledge that two people of equal education can receive the same information and arrive at differing conclusions. Then you fall into the trap of thinking, "Oh, this person thinks just like me!" and then getting a jolt when it turns out, in fact, No, they differ a little.

Gossip is toxic, and if you find yourself casting glances over your shoulder or otherwise making conversations you wouldn't want the subject to overhear, then you are in dangerous waters. It's all too human, of course, and everyone talks a little bit of smack here and there. Still, if the flaws and missteps of others are the core subject of discussion, you have my permission to change the subject, call it out for gossip, or otherwise stop. You don't have to high-road the group. Take your responsibility and own it as you move past it.

After all, if all someone can talk about is other people, you know darn well they do the same about you when your back is turned. "If you can't say something kind about someone, don't say anything at all" is a bit trite but holds enough water to use as a guide stone if not a hard and fast rule. It will quite simply not always be possible, but if the only things you can think of to say about someone are slights and jabs, why are they in your circle of friends to begin with? If the subject of your grievance is someone you are forced to acquaint yourself with, that's one thing, but keeping "friends" you do not respect is terrible form. Alpha Wolf theory is garbage, so don't think for one second there needs to be an Omega Wolf, the perpetual underdog a group bosses around but is still a valuable part of the pack? Nope.

Maybe you've been in an omega-type relationship with a group. Again, don't be anyone's fool. Some people like the role, but it is far less likely the group's underdog is there because they feel a need for submission than they are lonely or otherwise desperate for the company but never learned their worth. Always be careful who you trust, no matter how lonely or hyper-friendly you are feeling, and never let someone into your life too fast. At best, you become surrounded by tedious people you don't like; at worst, you get a bonafide Taker in your midst.

In my mad dash for branching out after high school, I ran into a real con man. Running long-term confidence scams, they stole from me, and I forgave them, and they stole from me again. I was naive and had never known an absolutely incorrigible liar and thief before. Rather than cast them out of my life altogether, I forgave them again. And, color me surprised, they stole from me again. So by the time I finally realized it was Fool Me Twice Shame On Me time, they had wormed their way into my friend's group and were stealing from them! Had I simply bounced the dude when he first wronged me, I would have saved all of us a good deal of misery.

I was provincial in the literal sense of the term: chronically under-traveled. I had never actually come across such a culprit, the occasional toy swiped by friends when young, notwithstanding! Unprepared for such behavior, I was completely disarmed. Of course, he was canny enough to target a demographic that mistrusted police. We were self-styled revolutionaries and rebels, radicals and outsiders-heaven forbid we condescend to call The Man. Had I a little perspective, I'd have picked up the phone the first time I noticed stuff disappearing and he failing to leave. That's why it can be so important to get out of your comfort zone, challenge your boundaries and push yourself through those things which intimidate you. Maybe I wouldn't have called the police for petty theft and trespass, but I sure would have had the backbone to get up in his face and make him leave. Bar the roommates from letting him into the apartment and make it stick. Such is hindsight, of course; all you can do is learn from those kinds of mistakes.

Teaching that kind of thing is difficult, if not impossible: how to guard against those who would steal, lie and cheat from within a circle of friends, or even a family group, is touchy. Teaching right from wrong and letting them know it applies to *everyone* no matter what is a good start, though no less an easy conversation. The more subtle life lessons can be harder to teach. Still, experience being the best crucible for personal truth, we can definitely start there. I have found no better way to give a young person perspective, relearn to appreciate differences when middle-aged, or stay forever-young as a senior than getting as far from the familiar as you can.

Traveling

Traveling is an excellent way to gain a new perspective. It can be so essential to keeping your horizons as wide as possible (both literally and figuratively) that I can't even call it Vacationing- it is too important. Traveling puts distance between you all that you know, not only your problems but your entire life, and often that increased vantage point is all it takes to reach a breakthrough. Removing the word 'vacation' also removes this insane push to spend as much money as we can while abroad. The traveling we do for personal development, even if it is just the joy of exploration, we call the Sojourn. This somewhat archaic word is nonetheless perfect for this book.

Get outside, yes, of course, but keep going until you are outside the familiar. Get outside the box. This can be as simple as taking a new route to work or as dramatic as flying across the globe. One of the surest ways to stagnate personally is to never leave your comfort zone. Well, homework time, leave that comfort zone because it goes by another name: A Rut! Ruts are the two groves carved into the middle of dirt roads. The same action repeated enough times creates a groove, making it hard to do anything else. Mix it up.

[Find your home on Google Earth, or the large-scale map of your choice, and draw a line, real or imagined, twenty miles around it. This is, on average, how far we move from home, an area perhaps not coincidentally as far as a typical person can walk in a day. Getting beyond this area should trigger the 'away' mindset. If you are already a mover and traveler, this radius may be more extensive. Now pin or mark the places you go all the time: school, work, grocery store, etc. The routine and your routes; you know you go the same way every time, and it is most likely the fastest, but consider other routes. Spend five or even ten minutes going out of your way, and you'll be surprised how little you know about those parts of town. In rural areas, this is more of an extended day-trip suggestion, but the concept is the same: get out of your comfort zone]

No car? Cash flow low? No problem; I road tripped all over this great big country of ours via greyhound, friends going my way and, once with a friend, even hitchhiked. The courageous spirit of youth and the relative safety of going with a friend made that leg of my summer of travel a freewheeling, spontaneous affair that taught me a lot about myself and the rest of the country. I was a little bit cliquish when young, very much personally identified with my little exclusive group, and casually derided those who didn't share my social stripe.

Well, putting myself at the mercy of strangers taught me Folks Is Folks Is All, a pithy expression I heard meaning people are people everywhere, most are friendly if not neutral, and gosh darn it, I had best get over myself if I am going to make the most of life. Sure enough, as soon as I dropped my pretentious facade and embraced those things we had in common, I had a much better time instead of focusing on what made us different. Because it's true: no matter if you're looking at a jet-setting business tycoon or subsistence farmer, strip away the Things, and we all have similar needs, drives, and fears. We always have far more in common with our fellow humans than not; forgive them for their small perceived failings because no one is perfect.

It can be easy to go through life facing backward; the wisdom of Those Who Forget The Past Are Doomed To Repeat It can be taken too far. Obsessing over what has happened and trying to recapture the past or hanging onto things that time is pulling away from both need to be guarded against. There's another archaic fifty-cent coffee shop word I like, Vicissitude, which means the Unavoidable Changes Over Time. You quite simply cannot fight the future. Things change, and if you do not want to be left behind, you have to change with them or at least keep up.

Now, being left behind in popular culture is OK. A preoccupation with being 'cool' really is best left to the young. Letting small things drift away is not only OK but necessary. We should expend energy keeping up with loved ones and close friends, not the Kardashians or whatever popular personality is attracting followers this decade. You will know who to look up to; your thoughts will naturally drift toward people who left an impression on you, and by analyzing those stray thoughts, you'll be able to tell if it's your brain warmly recalling a pleasant exchange or warning against hurt. You against past injury! Because bad habits creep up in relationships, too, and breaking those can be the hardest undertaking some of us attempt.

Break-Throughs

Growth, intentional and self-guided, is hard. I mentioned earlier that new behavior becomes a habit after 200 repetitions, now tempered with an understanding of just how much of an average that is. If we take to it fast, love it, and otherwise find ourselves swept away a little bit, we lose count after the first! Time flies when you're having fun, and in the ideal situation, you find something that inflames your passion so much it's hard to stop. If you cannot find something to inflame you so easily, then it's simple repetition until the desired action is automatic, or at least something you are resolved to doing. The 'rut' we try to break out of is a groove we wish to ride in if it's a positive habit. You train your brain with care to ensure our daily rituals are enriching our lives and not withering.

Fear Is the worst.

It has been fun watching the cultural awareness of fear's pivotal role in our lives dawn. From Roosevelt's "The only thing we have to fear is fear itself" line all the way up to how conquering your fear is the central plot point of endless movies, it seems like humanity is finally identifying that the biggest obstacle to personal growth is you. If it's not the actual fear of trying new things, looking silly, or getting hurt, but the perceived fear of failing, change, or doing something alone. Where this fear comes from is actually inconsequential: whether it's fearful parents, a few bad experiences, or just generic anxiety, once you analyze the risks and find them lacking, if you are still not making the moves you want to be making, then it's just Good Ol' Fashioned Basic fear and you can get past that.

The same way we write out or talk out all our big ideas now, as soon as you have determined what you want to do and that it is safe, you should get into the habit of acting on that idea. Impulsive is better than procrastinating much of the time, so make those bold moves and risk being wrong. Take the chance, take the leap of faith; spread those wings, and try to fly. Seriously, talking yourself out of great things happens to everyone. The only difference between many self-made millionaires and the rest of us is their ability to set aside doubt and blaze forward with no thought of failure. More important is picking yourself up and continuing when you get knocked down.

It is something you can practice: pushing through fear. Find a pool with a high dive. Get up there and jump. Cliff jumping is a heck of a lot more thrilling, but due to liability issues, it's not only hard to recommend but hard to find! Fear of falling is not universal, and if you are like me and never really had trouble with high dives, then find something vaguely terrifying (climbing, paintball, and sky-diving come to mind) and do it. Health and safety concerns considered, a bit of fear can be fun, and if it's just that rollercoaster or horseback tour you dread, then just do it. The more you get used to grasping the challenges that intimidate you head-on, the more capable you become at handling the more mundane ones. The more complex challenges you conquer, the more confident you become.

I had a close friend, trusted and capable, convince me to go backpacking through Wisconsin in the middle of winter. Like an extended Trust Fall, my life was in their hands as four of us overnighted the wilderness while hiking 20 miles in subzero temperatures. Having always been an avid camper, I was ready for some of it, but the myriad details you have to deal with were staggering. From freezing drinking water to supposedly thermal tested sleeping bags failing, it was one real hazard after another. While I can't expect every reader to have a friend who does such things For Fun, I am sure if you start asking around, you'll find someone to get you out of your comfort zone and into a wilderness, literal or figurative. Proving yourself against mental obstacles by conquering physical ones is a powerful tool. Still, you don't have to march into the woods in December or hurl yourself off a precipice to get a handle on things.

Phobias can be beaten with exposure therapy. Triggering the phobia a little at a time in short controlled sessions gives the mind a chance to experience the focus of intense fear without dread. Eventually, the irrational fear is nothing more than a memory. Decoupling the thoughts from the emotions they trigger takes time and repetition; see also: Practice. You should always be careful when interacting with the thought-emotion-behavior loop. This is where real, rapid personal advancement is possible. We have to just be sure we are advancing in a healthy direction!

Thoughts, Behavior & Emotions

The field of Cognitive Behavioral Therapy focuses on changing irrational and maladaptive behaviors or helping you develop a healthier relationship with them. You can use the field below to begin diagraming how Emotions, Thoughts, and Behavior interrelate. One is not even foundational to the other. All three follow each other like a locomotive attached to its own caboose. We can use this toolset as a way to begin deconstructing the elements of your life you wish to change and create new, healthier patterns in their place.

Once you have what you want to work on written down, fill in the other two blanks. Smoking is a Behavior, negative thinking is Thoughts, and depression is Emotions, etc. You begin to see how the interdependence of mind (thoughts), body (behavior), and spirit (emotions) really do interplay as a whole. Using these three facets as a tool, you can begin to zero in on exactly what sets you off and how you might short-circuit the undesired trait or at least change your relationship with it. Working with this triad is one of the ways we take a topic and look at it with dispassion, letting our emotions get validated without them running all over us.

Because of their origin within psychiatry, these tools are most powerful when practiced with a mental health professional. There is a stigma there, seeking help from a professional. That negative association is waning, and more and more, you see people embracing the concept. This idea that we can do it all alone, that needing help is a sign of weakness, is fading as the fallacy of Rugged Individualism is undone by the knowledge that none of us can go it alone. The famous 'pull yourself up by the bootstraps' line is a hilarious fraction of the whole quote "nobody can pull themselves up by their own bootstraps." The modern usage is a stunning inversion considering it came from the army; we are stronger together. We needed the tribe for all of humanity's time as hunter-gatherers, and we are still wired for intense social interactions just as much as we are strenuous physical activity.

As beneficial as it is to have guidance, such is not always available, and for the minor to medium stuff, it can be possible to self-administer. As ever when guiding yourself, you must guard against self-serving and self-deception. Getting lost in a hall of mirrors can be a fun distraction in a carnival but is a terrible place to get stuck in your own mind. More and more, public services and nonprofits are seeking to serve their communities' mental health, so if you do find yourself at wit's end and self-help is not enough, do a little research and make some calls. There are churches, synagogues and mosques, temples, shrines, and holy sites for the religious and spiritual if you need a little numinous support. Even if you left a church or organized service, may you yet find solace in other branches or off-shoots of the same tree? Well, who knows, find out? Explore and travel applies to your belief system, too: variations and new perspectives on one's core values being some of the most difficult, but with a very high cost-benefit ratio.

Shop it around.

People don't shop around for psychologists like they do doctors. I like how my spouse's folks handled when they moved across the country: they visited many churches of the same denomination before finding a priest they liked. Heck, many people just take the first professional assigned to them, but if you don't have a rapport with the people in charge of your well-being, then even routine care will be avoided. We are not talking about finding a doctor you would want to be buddies with, just someone on the same page. But only if that's important to you. You might find you like someone who is very different; their skill set is independent of friendship or even sympathy. Still, empathy and understanding are always crucial in a caregiver. More and more resources are being put toward mental health, too, so even if you think money is an obstacle, a little research will yield low and no-cost options in your area.

Because finances shouldn't stand in our way, but they often do. Not letting yourself fall into the Poor Me mentality can be crucial for changing your situation, monetarily or otherwise. While it is a lofty ideal to rise above such gross things as money, it becomes necessary to consider the food/shelter/water scale of needs.

Money

Let's not kid ourselves into thinking money buys happiness, but let's not try to insinuate it is easy to be happy with none, either. It might be possible, but the hardscrabble of getting your most basic needs met will likely take priority over more abstract concerns. You might grasp happiness on occasions, but the day-to-day struggle to survive tends to wear away joy. You don't want to fall into the trap of thinking you owe it to anyone to make as much money as you possibly can as much as you can. If you are given a choice between a medium-paying job that fulfills your spirit and a high-paying job that crushes your soul, you have to be able to make the choice that will benefit your whole persona. It is extremely liberating having an expendable income, but the stresses some jobs put a person through can be enough to break them.

I keep seeing the term Post-Capitalism tossed around in reference to the insane income inequality in the modern age but feel it may be a tab optimistic: it really doesn't look like capitalism is going anywhere anytime soon. Inflation and stagnant wages but a robust stock market have created the illusion of prosperity. Two incomes are not even a choice most families make, but a grim reality for all but the highest earners and penny-pinching. Most divorces cite money stresses as the primary factor in splitting up. I cannot even begin talking about American Medicine without wanting to spit nails. Going on and on about Money Not Buying Happiness can be a slap in the face to the working poor, but all the same, there is an element of truth to it. You can embrace joy no matter your situation, and the natural bliss of existence isn't in owning a lot of stuff.

Think about *why* you want the money. What are you buying with it? If it all comes down to Stuff and Things again, challenge yourself. This isn't even aimed at Richie Rich over there. The middle-class can be "house poor" when they live in a house they can barely afford the taxes on, and how about "shoe poor" as someone splurges on a shiny new pair of sneakers but then spends the rest of the month eating

Ramen? Once you begin looking at buying experiences and memories, investing in well-made instead of well-advertised clothes, and begin thinking of ways for your money to work for you, the waste and constant struggle fall away, and you begin to appreciate the difference between money and wealth.

If you find yourself coming up short every month, then it is time to make a budget. You need to get Back To Black, stay "out of the red." Did you know the term Black Friday, the frenzy of shopping that follows Thanksgiving's Thursday, is from the ink in a shopkeeper's ledger? Red for when the business is in debt and black for when it's turning a profit again? Stop seeing red, get on top of your finances and make a list of all your outflow- what I call Money Out. Where is it going, and why? You can learn quite a bit about yourself even if you are not broke.

Expenses (money out)	Income (money in)

What *are* your major expenses? How much are you spending on entertainment; are you distracting yourself from yourself? How much food; does EVERY meal have to be delicious all the time? What is your mortgage or rent; are you over-housed, with more space than you could ever use? If you are lucky enough to have these kinds of problems, I dare say the solution is easier than if it's a lack! Scaling down, doing more with less, and embracing a more minimal lifestyle will all put money back in your pocket, though, and the copious consumption encouraged by modern life is easy to avoid once it has been identified as such.

71

My grandparents were both on different sides of the middle-class: one lived in the same house she'd raised the kids in, a residential neighborhood in the state's biggest metropolitan area. The others lived on a lake, having bought, remodeled, and sold a few homes in between. One had a savings account, the other owned a diverse portfolio of stocks, bonds, and other investments. Both came up in hard times from poverty, and both were even of similar ancestry. Sure, luck played its role: both granddads served in WW2, but one on a base back home and one in a unit which suffered 100% casualties; one side is riddled with depression and anxiety, the other seemingly not. But overall, the reason one side wound up in a lake house worth over a million and the other in a quaint if not drafty urban two-story came down to thinking and vision.

Both sides were unwilling to take what was given, worked hard, and had strong morals. It was the vision, the house-on-the-lake side seeing how it could be done and doing it. Not everyone will have had the same experiences with affluence and the lack thereof growing up, but you can always learn to think in terms of investments and money working for you—the rich seldom sock all their money into an idle saving account, wealth-generating wealth a very real thing. Getting enough money together to start that process is the subject of entire fields of research! Let's stick to knowing when you are being pandered to and when you are getting reliable information for now.

Advertisements Deconstructed

Identifying when you are being advertised to has gotten harder in this modern life, as corporate entities can literally track us, spy on us, and tailor ads just to us. It was bad enough when we were simply emotionally manipulated, but now we're being swamped by precise, metric-driven come-ons made from our very own likes and dislikes, location, and prior purchases. It has never been more important to not only pinch your pennies but be careful what you are basing your purchasing decisions on. Your awareness of your train

72

of thought, to not let any new idea go unchallenged, will serve you well here.

This can be as literal as thinking something and then immediately analyzing where you heard it or learned it or rereading an old journal entry and realizing it is something your mom used to say all the time. Are you reaching for that higher light or letting the past determine your future? I am not sure if it was only my dad trying to shoot down my brother and me wanting new toys from the TV, but one of the first things I remember my father teaching me was how advertisements try to trick you, fool you, or otherwise are not to be trusted. At that time, he was waiting for an ad to come on of a toy we never play with anymore. Still, as time went on, I focused on false excitement, hyped-up passion, and fake enthusiasm.

I still have zero patience with ads (I will be curt, bordering on rude, to aggressive salespeople), but here's why: everyone and everything is selling something, sometimes! It can be as innocent as your friend trying to get you to go do something you are unsure about or as mortal as a cult trying to lure you in, but knowing when you are being pandered to, having your emotions played and manipulated in any way is a powerful tool. It will make sure you do not get sucked into unhealthy relationships. Abusers always have to sell themselves back to their victims, that is, until the target of their abuse gives up entirely and becomes a willing host to a parasitic individual.

I once read that some of the folklore around vampires was more about giving people the tools to deter confidence-scam con artists than supernatural horrors. Those horrible individuals who would sweep into your life and offer deals too good to be true or sudden, passionate romances really *do* have to be invited in. Once in your life, a selfish, always-taking type of person can bleed you dry and make you a shell of your former self. In a long-term co-dependent relationship, the abused can even go on to become a monster themselves, acting out the same transgressions against others that they were subjected to.

73

To go from commercials to vampires might seem a broad contextual leap. Still, once we look at it conceptually, we realize in both cases you have one greater force trying to woo a smaller one, looking to suck the money (or blood) from you. Stand For Something Or You'll Fall For Anything keeps coming up, and it is only by having a system of belief or philosophy of action that we can hope to keep our wits about us as so many factors and influences try to buffet you this way and that. When your anchor cable snaps and your ship is set adrift on the storm-tossed seas, it is important to have a guide star or lodestone to guide the way back.

Axioms

An Axiom is an immutable truth, something true eternally. I love trying to find Universal Truisms for the modern age as any broad declarative statement usually breaks under the burden of reality. In this fantastically complex universe, there is very little we can say for certain about everything. Once we pare down what we know from what we want, we are often left with something cold and indifferent. "Life is not fair," "nobody owes you anything," and "bad things happen to good people" seem like cold, hard lessons, and it is no surprise some will turn away from those harsh truths and try to find solace in a lie. It is possible to find a certain amount of solace in that kind of thinking, if not comfort, then at least a sort of predictability.

Religious teachings are full of supposedly immutable truths, but the fact of the matter is that the best of intentions often fail to take into account the complexities of a situation, to say nothing of how any given situation can develop. While often attributed to Churchill or Eisenhower, a German field commander, Moltke the Elder, is first quoted as saying, "No plan of operations extends with certainty beyond the first encounter with the enemy," and it applies to peacetime, too. A plan is a guideline, but as soon as you begin, you're going to be confronted with details you never thought of, conflicts you couldn't have anticipated, and find a strict adherence to the recipe for life impossible to achieve.

Expecting the unexpected is why it is essential to remain flexible. Having clearly explored your philosophies and beliefs, when you are confronted with sudden, unexpected choices, you can take a step back and appreciate how the sacred texts or hallowed philosophies you subscribe to intend your posture and stance to be. Even if they never came out and addressed your particular issue, there is usually something similar. While it would have been impossible for the prophets and sages of the ancient world to predict all the changes wrought by 21st-century living, you can usually adapt a way forward in keeping with the spirit of your chosen faith.

You need to have words you can believe in for your mind to use. With very few exceptions, words are thoughts, and their power cannot be underestimated. After all, when confronted with the Honor Thy Father and Mother edict in the face of a notorious child abuse case from my youth, the Bible teacher I asked stated unequivocally that those parents are not honoring their children, making the commandment null and void. I wonder now how many curious kids got a different answer when questioning authority?

Being skeptical is often seen as the death of belief or the absence of hope, but the opposite is true as long as it's not taken to a nihilistic degree. You have to love something quite a bit to pick it apart and challenge it; self-love is challenging yourself as much as it is supporting yourself. Wanting something to be true shouldn't blind you to the truth- always explore other possibilities. But neither should you throw the baby out with the bathwater when it looks like things don't go right. I never felt closer to my country than when I was protesting some of its practices I felt strongly about. Balance is never-ending; finding accord with universal truths in a constantly changing universe is challenging but not impossible. Just know that we all stumble sometimes. Nobody is perfect, but even forgiveness should have its limits.

When you grow, when you reach those highest ideals, it can be tempting to put your go all-in with generosity. Once you get into the spirit of giving, it can be tempting to give until it hurts and then give some more.

The Spaces Between

The real measure of virtue is how you behave when nobody's watching. Another common pitfall for the intrepid self-developer is those quiet moments in-between. Idle minutes here and there where we're at ends as to what to do with ourselves can be the downfall of an otherwise steady routine. Again, it doesn't have to be anything as obvious as secret binge drinking or midnight treats. Self-talk when alone can differ dramatically from when we are with people or alone. Indeed, this feeling of inadequacy when alone can drive many people to keep friends long after their toxicity has been revealed.

Hobbies, any kind of pastime, is a guard against those idle times becoming a problem. Without something to do with our hands, many of us have become addicted to our phones, literally designed to keep us trapped in endorphin loops. Having something else to pick up and mess around with is vital in this day and age. If arts and crafts aren't your thing, have you considered small engine repair? No, I am not joking. Animal training or puzzles? You might have hated puzzles as a kid, but have you tried one (with a really cool picture!) in your adult life? While I never got into them as a kid, I was pleasantly surprised at just how oddly satisfying completing a puzzle is as a (somewhat) mature adult human.

While having something to show for it has a real benefit to the psyche, don't think everything you do has to have a tangible output. Especially in a weak economy, it can be tempting to try and monetize our every minute, turning hobbies into side hustles, or even just working three or four jobs at once. After a certain point, just having fun is its own reward. As long as you don't disappear into escapism or waste all your time, anything you are doing that's not stirring yourself up into unhealthy habits is good.

If you reached this point in life with no pastimes, interests you can follow up on, or hobbies to speak of, search for it. Look for one, actively seek out a stimulating experience and see what it leads to. Maybe you have one that fails to inspire you anymore. Going and finding another might be just what you need to rekindle the spark from it or get you off in another direction. Museums are rooted in the word Muse, after all, and any kind of gallery, exhibition, or collection can be interesting if you go in with an open mind.

Sure, Stamp Collecting might sound boring, but it gets into history, art, politics, and typography. Typography itself sounds tedious at first, but I had an absolutely obsessed friend. While I can't say I ever got into it too much, I learned what a serif was, the terror of poor kerning, and how to spot a lousy font before it's too late. If you consider the sheer amount of information available these days, no amount of intellectual curiosity should be left unsatisfied. Feeding the brain is good, and if we are seeking whole-body balance, then feeding the body should be taken with just as much consideration.

Sustenance

I cannot help you outline a path toward robust and vertical growth without making you consider what you are putting in your body. The multi-billion dollar dieting and nutrition industry aren't all hawking snake oil, as the You Are What You Eat thing is not just a trite figure of speech but an axiom we can depend on. Eating processed, artificial food will leave you feeling sluggish; the calories burn too fast, so you feel hungry sooner, too. Because by now I hope you have a healthy diet. It can cover books all to itself; I'll only say that you must consider it as hard as you do exercise and positive thinking: foundational. Foundational in the way of "footings," the deeply driven corners that hold the very foundation in place.

Roots in the very literal sense of absorbing nutrients and roots in the sense of how your parents eat are how you eat *unless* you have consciously moved away from their patterns.

77

I don't think there are many families who don't have a grandparent or great-grandparent that has died of organ failure related to diet. The last century ate terribly, and society is only now coming around to nutritional balance and a science-based approach to eating. Some folks will go gluten-free even if they aren't Celiac because the modern diet is saturated with it. Intermittent fasting works for so many because the meals we eat are so calorie rich. This topic is based on personal physiology and genetics, environment, and background. I can only advise caution in making dramatic long-term changes without talking to a professional who knows your medical history. You don't want to try fasting if you are pre-diabetic, and someone with IBS isn't going to want to do a juice cleanse without a bit of supervision.

As we move into the later stages of personal development, you begin to consider not just where you are going but where you have been. The path before you might be a mystery, but you have every bit of control over the trail behind you. As we navigate our way through life with love in our hearts, it becomes essential to leave a matching legacy. It is only through respect of others and their experience that we avoid the unfortunately sometimes truism The Road To Hell Is Paved With Good Intentions. I hated this expression until I understood the speaker is saying you can't just smile, pray and hope for the best- you have to act. Be the change you want to see in the world. This is doubly true in self-love: take the next step, BE the change you want in your life, or it will never happen.

A plant never stops reaching towards the light. It's like an expression I heard when I was young that has resonated louder and louder the older I get: "the moment you stop growing, you start dying." Maybe a *tad* dramatic, but the stagnation of our inner waters and Zero Growth is a pretty bleak existence. Remember to take new phases of personal growth incrementally, step by step, and day by day. Making new positive habits is every bit like breaking old bad ones. It takes patience and tenacity, a mind for long-term thinking, and perhaps most important of all, a willingness to get back on the path when (not if) you stray.

Sometimes it might seem like you are just spinning your wheels. Still, just like gaining traction on an icy surface, you will be just spinning your wheels at first. Still, once you get the knack, you begin rocking back and forth until suddenly you're rocketing forward. It might be hard going at times, but the result is always worth it.

Chapter 3: Leaf

What you give the future, your produce, whether acorn, flower, or fruit. Do you cast shade or let in more light? Are we loving ourselves at the exclusion of others?

Once we begin to grow as humans and become aware of how our actions affect us and the world around us, we begin to wonder what kind of heritage we are leaving the planet. It doesn't even have to be anything as profound as written works or well-adjusted children (though it might) but as simple as the impression we leave on people and general demeanor projected outward. Do our branches grasp and claw for others to latch onto, stealing the sun from those around you, or do we dig deep and stretch skyward, offering shade to the heated and light to the darkness? Here's where the plant metaphor breaks down because most plants will crowd each other out, tightly packed trees killing one another until only the biggest and strongest survive, which sounds like a famous incorrect axiom: Only The Strong Survive.

...and Anyway, We're Not Wolves

This 'survival of the fittest' thinking is not just a misinterpretation of Darwin's theory of evolution but leads to another human behavior fallacy of the modern age: Alpha Wolf. First, let's look at that Darwin quote.

Only The Strong Survive is a gross oversimplification of evolution, the fact being any creature who survives long enough to pass on their genes survives, and what gets passed on is by no means a guarantee of it being great. Look no further than the peacock, whose ridiculously long tail feathers are absolutely crucial to a peahen but don't do the male any favors in the 'hiding from prey' for even 'medium distance flying' category. Just like flashy tail feathers can help make babies but hinder practically everything else, there are human behaviors that have perpetuated into the modern age that never did any of your ancestors any favors.

"Alpha Wolf" thinking is bogus right down the line: the naturalist who first penned those observations dedicating the rest of their career to emphasizing the correct model of wolfpack behavior. It turns out that the wolf pack being observed was a collection of wolves from different packs jammed into a small zoo enclosure. Natural packs are simply parents and their offspring: A wolf that tries to dominate the others gets driven from the group. It doesn't ascend to a leadership role. Those original observations made in the Basel Zoo of Switzerland by Rudolf Schenkel in 1947 were even retracted later that year, noting that wolves in the wild would be led by a mated pair. Still, it was ignored in favor of the theory, which seemed to validate jerks to continue being jerks.

It can be so easy to fall into a habit of domination if we are allowed to. It feels good to be followed, and we are told from a young age that leadership is one of the best roles one can aspire to. Leadership must be tempered with compassion and genuine respect for the people putting their direction in your hands. If the only reason you wanted to be the leader was to boss people around, you are going to have a bad time. Great leaders lead by example, and it takes approximately two minutes to tell when a new boss or supervisor is a petty tyrant or disciplined manager. Sometimes you won't know until the hammer drops on you, and there's no accounting for the actions of others. All we can do is be sure we are beyond reproach more times than not and steer clear of those who would tear us down.

Stand Strong

By reflecting on the forces around us, the influences, and all prevailing factors, it will be possible to determine when we have been done wrong and when fortune has simply frowned on us. No hot streak lasts forever, and even the strongest, tallest tree one day withers. You have to assume that sometimes you will not win, that you are not always right, and your poop stinks. That colorful expression is one we forget as adults. We eat so much crow as kids, ignorant and naive we learn and strive, but even as adults, there are holes in our understanding you could throw a cat through. While I doubt most adults are thinking, "I am never wrong," the defensive, reactionary human can definitely fall into the habit of never admitting fault.

A really great quote on the realities of perseverance and a real winners attitude comes from Star Trek, Captain Picard's words ring as true in the real world as it does in the fictional 24th century: "It is possible to commit no mistakes and still lose. That is not a weakness; that is life." How often do we find ourselves flailing at life's injustices when we should be getting over it and moving forward? Mommy and daddy might have tried to make for an equanimous house, and you might have been lucky enough to find an employer who rewards hard work and keeps a level playing field. But for the most part, all things being equal, all things are not equal, and sometimes you're going to get a flat, caught out in the rain, or otherwise wind up with egg on your face.

How you react to adversity is far more important than how you react when everything is fine.

"When the going gets tough, the tough get going" should flash across your field of vision whenever you feel like quitting. Evolutionary biologists insist humanity's greatest physical asset is our stamina. Not claws, armor, or spines like the beasts around us; our drive and ability to outlast which won out over the eons. Once we put these fantastic brains to a task, we can doggedly pursue it until it drops from exhaustion. If you can learn to apply that unrelenting tenacity toward your goals and dreams, then I dare say there's little you couldn't archive.

What We Make

The impression you leave on the world is either beneficial or detrimental. There's not really any room for neutrality, as society itself is the final arbiter. Many of us seek out hermetic lifestyles, looking for isolation and seclusion. We find our true selves and, if introverted, recharge. But isolation is largely a myth. Our mutual interdependency is as literal as sharing the plant and as abstract as humans being social creatures. Unless you actually do go off and live in a cave somewhere, you'll always have social interactions at least, actual products and creations at most. Considering what you are doing for a living measured against your beliefs and values is essential.

Once more, you might not even be plagued with a moral dilemma on par with my dad, who was a Tool and Die Maker by trade. He went to school to get out of Viet Nam and raised his kids anti-war; anti-war is also pro-soldier, he was quick to point out, his own father's Purple Heart and PTSD proof of that. In his line of work, you make parts for clients, and at some point, he was asked to make a part for a missile system of some kind. He was no avowed pacifist, and he made the part, but it certainly haunted him a bit. In the future, he would even ask if the employer took military contracts or not. Even I, when looking for small gig work to fill in some spare moments, found a weird "voice acting" type of task that actually turned out to be training drone AI to recognize human words! No thanks.

Major stuff, yes. How about we take a second to look at the product of your passing moments that you leave behind where you simply walk? Remember, every stranger really is a friend you haven't met yet. While not wholly accurate, consider how often that random person is met later, or you get hired with that one guy you pass on the road every day. You can take a self-interested mentality and be kind only to make the day easier for you or use an altruistic mindset and consider it as throwing good vibes into the universe. Whichever way you look at it, there's no reason to go through life casting shade. Self-love means you don't have to throw shade, cut others down and one-up everyone around you because you no longer need to cast others down to raise yourself up.

I have heard that term used, and it fits so well into the framework we are using. I just couldn't resist- Don't Cast Shade means to stop tearing everything apart, complaining, and being negative right off the bat. It means trying to be optimistic at most and just not being a prickly pear, at least. You don't need to slap a smile on your face and beam; just watch your tone and meaning. I have a wicked cynical streak I've had to curtail, my sense of humor cutting and acidic if I don't watch my tongue. While we don't want to self-censor, we want to let everything that comes to mind out while not offending. This is also audience-based: some of my more bawdy friends will laugh at anything and have the same ability to make fun of things we care deeply about that I do. It is a great release to spend time with these people, cracking on life and laughing until our sides hurt. Because to us, humor is a coping mechanism though we understand it's not everyone's.

All too often, we forget to laugh. It is easy to get stuck and wind up in a rut. Pushed and pulled around the workplace and unable to vent, it can be easy to get home and find ourselves lashing out at those around us. Lashing out at loved ones is the final measure of when we've begun to take the safety and security of home for granted or a learned behavior we must undo. Those that love us don't deserve to be the final resting place of our anger and frustration, and we must always guard against such unworthy reactions.

We can make sure and get the most out of this book by monitoring what is hindering our self-love. Ask questions; if you draw a blank, use the notes after the question to prompt you.

1. What do I hope to get from this book? Self-develop *what*?
2. What will my success look like? Set goals.
3. What is preventing me from achieving this? Set aside time, create milestones.
4. Who supports me? Not only people but pets and role models.

Love Is a Verb

Making a love that lasts is work. Make no mistake: there is no Credits Roll, Happily Ever After. Marriage is not an endpoint, and any love will die if you don't nurture it. Long-term happiness with a partner, either passionate or platonic, is something you have to work at. There will be times of frustration with anyone, especially those people we let into our lives the deepest. As long as we are acknowledging the humanity of those around us, the occasional sour day won't jeopardize the whole deal. If we fail to regulate our negative emotions in a healthy way, however, what may have been a healthy, lasting bond gets weak and dies. Working at love means giving sometimes; no partner likes to be used, and we all deserve respect.

Some people really get a great deal of satisfaction serving the ones they love and will give and give long after many of us have stopped. There are those who take and take, usually choosing partners of the giving type. Both types have to stop and ask themselves to what degree their fulfillment comes at the expense of another, even if the other is themselves!

When we first moved in together, my spouse started the tradition of kissing goodbye. For work, out to the store, even just walking the dog: if you are leaving the house, you get a kiss. In the beginning, I didn't think it was a big deal and even caught myself getting annoyed when I was a few steps out the door and had to come back for kisses. Now, it is I who gives the kisses, and we laugh when it's repeated ("Oops, forgot something, back to the house...") or otherwise happens a few times in a row. But when we had a child, it is a practice I am glad to have taught them through demonstration: now I get to kiss them both.

It's a simple thing. When I began working from home, it became possible to re-embrace a little bit of my night owl tendencies. I can and will stay up late working on something if I get caught up in it. Even when I can stay up late, sometimes I elect to go to bed with them. You have to make time, choose the little things, and remember special days (get and maintain a personal calendar if you can't remember stuff like that). Because it really is the little things, as long as you got the big stuff covered! Kisses and random hugs, little everyday displays of affection are the mortar, but miss the big events at your peril, too.

Taking a loved one for granted happens to the best of us; all we can hope to do is snap out of it and make sure the other person knows we care. Remember why they got tangled up with you in the first place and grow with you. How we deal with life's slings and arrows tells us more about ourselves than how we manage good days. While "You have to love yourself before anyone else can love you" is hopelessly simplistic and quite simply not true, having a strong inner resolve, mental discipline, and at least some level of self-worth is crucial to your overall well-being.

As I hope you see by now, self-love is no exception. Any amount of time we spend on self-discipline, self-care, and self-analysis will be returned in a stronger will, more flexible imagination, and genuine patience for others. Don't go overboard and become an egotist, of course, but strike a balance between worth and room to grow. Loving the self can be as simple as giving yourself permission to take a nap or as grand as going on a personal retreat. Men, I have it on very good authority that a pedicure is an experience any gender can enjoy. Ladies, you've heard of the Man Cave- if you have the room, why not a Girl Grotto? At the end of the day, if you don't make time for yourself, nobody else will. Even those closest to you don't know what you need in this area, which is why cultivating the self is so important.

People may love you, but only you know where The Light is; only you know what you need.

What Doesn't Bend Breaks

When most trees are grown in greenhouses, they grow to a certain height and topple over. It was discovered that wind buffeting the three forces it to grow deeper roots and a stronger trunk, making its limbs stronger and more flexible as its branches. This image, more than anything, should be the primary inspiration: how we respond to the forces beyond our control makes us strong. We can get blown down or learn to stand strong. We can wither in a drought or sink our roots down until we find sustenance. Everyone suffers; life is going to dish out pain *and* pleasure. The objective of healthy mental discipline is Not focusing on the negative so much we drown out the positive. Yes, we are aware of those slings and barbs because we seek to avoid them, but we do so by seeking the good and enriching, moving toward that instead.

How do you cope? When your mind is rebelling, maybe fixating on something out of your control or dragging you back into dark broodings, how do you force a shift?

Drugs and Alcohol

I think for most Americans, and from what I can see most of humanity, Booze is the number one social lubricant and coping mechanism. There is such a strong level of abuse it's not something many even think of as a negative. To say nothing of how psychologically unhealthy it is to reach for a bottle every time life gets you down. This is here as a heads up: more than one or two drinks a day really isn't good for your body or your brain. If you drink to intoxication every time you drink, that is a problem. But even just three or four servings can loosen you up too much, make your thinking sloppy and leave you in a depressed state. Technically, alcohol is a depressant due to how it affects the body, so even the 'happy drunk' lowers their metabolism and puts unnecessary stresses on the body.

Marijuana has medical properties, sure, but are those people using it to treat mental conditions doing so in conjunction with psychiatric counseling and therapy? Not usually. There are a few cities that have decriminalized hallucinogens. There is promise in low doses of some of them used in conjunction with medical practitioners to curb addictions and even cure PTSD. Still, again, outside of the realm of careful clinical supervision, it's less therapeutic and more self-indulgent. There have been sacred drug use in almost every religion you can think of, so seeking drugs out for enlightenment or just personal exploration can be tempting.

In terms of a self-help manual, this topic is basically off the table beyond a warning against it. The possibility of a negative interaction or serious problems springing out of even well-intentioned suggestions is just too darn high.

If it alters your brain, you shouldn't be doing it all the time. Exceptions exist, of course; a buddy of mine has a family member that's bipolar manic depressive. Without a careful regime of meds and psychoanalysis, he gets self-destructive ideation and manic, uncontrollable mood swings. Put another way, without drugs, he tried to end his own life a few times. On them, he's musical, funny and loves life. So it can be hard to make the broad sweeping declaration that Drugs Are Bad. You have to be smart. But as a coping mechanism, drugs are terrible, being far too invasive and damaging, to say nothing of expensive, and you now have an external power over you. Far better to trigger as many of the pleasure-causing hormones and neural chemicals naturally as you can. Loving yourself feels great! Far better than the alternative.

Exercise

Back to physical activity, I know, but it is unbelievable how many people think they can cheat this one. The benefits are well documented, and the effects of not doing anything so disastrous it scarcely worth mentioning again! However, when the going gets tough and life is weighing you down, little else gets you up as consistently as some strenuous activity. If you are stressed, upset, or depressed, pushing yourself past your comfort zone and "feeling the burn" will get things back into alignment.

Don't burn yourself out; going harder when you are upset can be dangerous if you lose touch with your body, and it's easy to do when you are focusing on what's troubling you. Breath, focus, feel the forces squeezing you loosen up as the blood and breath flows through you. Imagine letting go, loosening up, and opening wide. Using exercise as therapy works so much better when you couple it with positive visualizations and self-talk. You're not jogging (for instance) away from problems but toward solutions. You're not only forcing bad mojo out by doing yoga but breathing in love, too. You have no control over some things, and letting yourself let go of those is a lifelong process.

Talk

Discuss things that matter to you. As simple as it sounds, I am including those you don't *want* to talk about specifically. I constantly remember this one because as much as I like to talk, laugh, and have a good time, there is also a high degree of Avoidance. I'll quite simply try not to think about things that bother me; I've traced it back to good old-fashioned mental defense mechanisms kicking in and the unfortunate result of having learned how to control my thinking to some degree. Suppose I find myself avoiding certain topics either in my thoughts or conversations. In that case, I have to force the issue, as it were, by willing myself to confront it directly. Don't let it all bottle up and burst. It is called "dumping on" for a reason, as in "oh gosh, I didn't mean to dump all over you; I just haven't had anyone to talk to about this yet!" If the person is not ready, willing, and able to take a sudden emotional download, they can feel burdened or on the spot. Letting those perplexing, sometimes conflicting thoughts out a little bit at a time is every bit like a pressure release valve on a pressure cooker; squeaking out a little bit at a time makes sure you don't blow up! Even if the company you keep steers the conversations back into more familiar waters, you have expressed yourself and made it known you're not afraid of going deep.

Clean

When the going gets tough, the tough get Cleaning. Why do you think most grandma's houses are always neater than most young people's? Experience. No matter how untidy they grow up, by the time most of us reach our golden years, it is apparent a clean living space equals a well-ordered mind, too. Well-traveled individuals clean the house before leaving on a trip, coming home to a clean home as important as packing your underwear. When you find yourself at your wit's end, throw yourself into deep cleaning your home.

It's nervous energy well spent and an investment in the immediate future. At some point, of course, you must stop. Balance, remember balance? I think many of you who are reading this book might Over Clean and never let yourself sit still as you putter around the house. Far be it from me to demand the tireless homemaker ever stop making their home as perfect as possible but is it driving you to distraction? Are you missing out on socializing because you can't stop trying to clean up the party *during* the party? On the other hand, do your parties completely trash the space because nobody is doing any precleaning? Suffice to say, the time you spend cleaning is almost always productive, so it is as good of a way to blow off steam as any.

Produce

This is what we think of as arts and crafts, but far more inclusive. Lawn Care was the outward expression of self for previous generations of men, Cars, and Careers too. Some still practice those old status symbols, but this modern age offers men and women both long-term projects the other was denied in decades past, and so many more. Men can quilt, garden, and crochet if they want to. Women can tinker, hunt, and do home maintenance. Besides the breaking down of useless gender roles, 21st-century living offers all sorts of pastimes and projects not even dreamed of when I was young.

Consider your craft, remembering to keep that word as open-ended as possible.

Reading is good, great even, but if you're a voracious reader, have you considered writing? Critique or editing? A lifetime of literacy has given you a sharp eye for prose; might you be able to put that to use elsewhere?

3-D Printing is a wild and wildly time-consuming hobby, with real monetary possibilities if you just *have* to monetize everything. There's a programming side to that one, which is a whole other obsession/hobby: software and coding. While people get intimidated by the very idea, if you have an eye for details and a mind for rules, learning a programming language is definitely something that can turn into a career, and many an amateur coding enthusiast has gone through the exquisite pain and pleasure of realizing they can make more money at their hobby but then lamenting as their cherished pastime becomes a job instead of a passion!

Not sure? I promise the whole wide world has been bored, at ends as to what to do with itself and over the eons and multitudes, someone somewhere with your particular aptitude and interests has started doing something you'd love. Piano Tuning, nowadays that includes Instrument Repair, is neat and leads to Organ Tuning and Repair. Do you want to talk about moving parts? Even just watching a video on massive, building-sized air-powered old organs is cool. Yes, at the point of simply not knowing what might interest you, it is a good idea to head to the internet (or public library!) and just start searching. Stamp Collecting has hobbies within hobbies, as does Fly Fishing and Model Railroading- deeply complex activities that you can join at the entry-level and then follow as many rabbit holes down as you care to.

Anything is like that if you Geek Out on it hard enough: you can get into the details, learning all there is to know about something offers its own kind of satisfaction. This type of deep knowledge used to be 'nerdy,' something you only revealed to close friends. Everyone is pretty much OK with whatever floats your boat in this era, so it is far easier to find interest groups and get people talking about their passions.

While it is overall a good thing to do what you love for a living, the loss of control over personal projects has been enough to make many visionaries choose to work in obscurity rather than let go of creative freedom.

What a delightful dilemma to be in, though: forced to choose between getting paid to do what you love, albeit to somebody else's design, or continue doing what you are doing? Does the painter who's just found a patron love the craft itself or the self-expression? It will depend on how specific your muse is.

Are you driven by a singular vision, the image of what you want to create burning so bright you could almost reach out and touch it? Or is the act of doing just as if not more important? I've known a graphic artist to jump up and down in excitement when they land a huge client only to jump up and down in excitement a few years later when they build up the courage to leave that cushy job for the unpredictable but totally free life of the working artist.

Knowing your heart, trusting that you know best for yourself, and acting on those inner needs will make sure you waste as little time slaving under conditions you hate as possible. We have all heard the stories of CEOs and other Master's of Industry that chuck it all and live a simpler, happier life afterward. As long as your needs are met and you have a nice little cushion besides, the rest is a pile of gold you may never use. Besides, if the super-rich keeps getting richer, pretty soon being wealthy is going to be about as popular as being noble during the French Revolution. Which is all to say, don't let the pursuit of wealth become the end in itself; remember why you wanted the liquid assets in the first place. Because at the end of the day, what you produce will outlast you.

Your Seed

Not as literal as offspring and not as abstract as the impression you leave on the world around you, the seed, in this case, is your legacy. Sometimes a literal inheritance you leave behind for your kids; it also includes intangibles like attitude and work ethic. It is also attitudes, beliefs, and behaviors. Your parents gave you a template of actions and thoughts- what are you modeling for yours? If not kids, the people who respect you wind up mirroring you. That's a fact of human behavior: you begin using the words of people you want to be closer to, repeating actions and inevitably thoughts. Knowing your role in that equation is powerful, and inspiration to be better and knowledge any self-cultivation you might succeed in won't have been in vain.

So much of what we learn is absorbed passively. While it is absolute when we are growing up, it is more and more up to us to consciously adopt new behaviors as adults. When we are young, we unconsciously take on the words and mannerisms of our family and friends as we strive to make an identity of our own. If we hold our parents in contempt, we want all of our learned behavior to be based on the friends and loved ones we surround ourselves with. Often, humans being humans winds up being just a different version of the same situation. The dressings changed, but the roles and power dynamics the same: abused kids go into violent gangs like clockwork. If heavy-handed grown-ups raised you, chances are good you will grow up to hit your own kids. Violence gets normalized, and the next generation is raised with corporal punishment. Never mind that no modern research supports hitting your kids, "I was raised that way, and I turned out fine" becomes the rational, with no thought to, "well, maybe I didn't turn out as fine as I thought."

To escape the unhealthy past, you have to work for it.

Nothing good comes easy. In fact, by adulthood, you should be extremely skeptical of anyone offering easy answers and simple solutions. Even psychiatric medicine is usually taken under the supervision of a professional—regular check-ins and occasional rebalancing are necessary for anything more than a simple prescription. As your journey progresses, it can be tempting to grow complacent and drop some of these best practices, but I urge you to be vigilant. It is those moments when we are weakest we have to be sure of our path.

Forest

Far from a self-contained unit, the human-animal is a group, a social body whose total is greater than the sum of its parts. Like it or not, every great thing humans have achieved has been together. Nobody built a rocket and landed on the moon without hundreds, thousands of people working together and no farmer sows, reaps, and tills alone. When we reach out, branches extending upward and roots tapping resources, we do it as an aggregate mass. As independent as you may be, there's electricity, roads, and builders, at least, an entire infrastructure that exists just so you can exist comfortably.

Are you a member of any groups? If not, where does your primary source of socialization come from? Is it an equal give and take of socialization or a one-way street of being a wallflower or conversation domination? Remember that introvert and extrovert are a False Dichotomy, which means people are likely to insist you have to be one or the other when the answer is always somewhere in the middle. At best, a False Dichotomy is an oversimplification, and at worst, it is intentionally crafted to persuade. In people's hurry to find a trail through the wilderness, it's possible to miss the forest for the trees. Those who might try to point to a fork in the road usually lead you down the wrong one.

You see the False Dichotomy used so much because it's so effective. "Do you want to save the environment or cost these families these jobs!" and more recently, "Do you want police reform or no police!" There's a middle ground; there's always a way through, and seldom is anything truly yes or no. If nothing else, you learn to parse the multitude of options and understand that there are as many ways forward as there are human beings. Accepting another's point of view is not a weakness if it is better.

Where We Go From Here

Go With The Flow or Fight The Future? In the push and pull of Sticking To Your Guns and Turning Over A New Leaf, will you thrive or wither? Ah-ha, you spotted a possible false dichotomy but fear not. You can both wither and thrive, drop limbs and grow new ones, shed leaves to regrow them again.

It can never be a bad thing to say I Was Wrong. We should always be growing, always seeking to be the most positive influence on the world as we can. Being able to say you were wrong is also being able to take responsibility for your actions. Sometimes the hardest part is making amends, even if it is just an I'm Sorry. Just know that in the realm of interpersonal communication, the words "I'm Sorry" come with an implicit promise: 'I will try not to repeat the behavior.'

An apology is ONLY enough if the offending behavior is not repeated. Those habits and manners which led to the transgression should be changed, or you risk future apologies ringing hollow.

Personal development isn't a destination, but a means to an end. Decide where you want to grow and go. You can read nothing in a book that will give you all the answers, but you can use them as guide stars, a neutral third party offering you new ideas. It can be easy to dismiss idealists as unrealistic, but most of us are well aware sticking to our values means an endless series of compromises as we tirelessly inch toward our goals. You cannot give up, stop striving and growing, or on those occasions that the universe seems to align, a clear path forward opens up, and you can leap forward and get missed. You have to keep your eyes on the prize because it is not always the big meeting or long-term project that wins you what you want. Just as often, we can surge ahead during one of those random occurrences, a freak match-up or run-in when doors open and opportunities arise. When you find an unexpected side-path, if you have already told yourself you've failed, you won't go down it.

Had you given up, had you decided it was impossible, you'd have missed it. You Miss 100% of the Shots You Don't Take, and that means: act. Take the chance. Don't gamble away your savings on get-rich schemes but don't let yourself miss out on legitimate investments, either. Risk a broken heart by pursuing your most authentic desires and raise again if and when you are broken-hearted.

We can rise above mean circumstances. We can grow upwards while not forgetting what's behind us. Knowing there IS greener grass out there, we can keep seeking greener pastures, and knowing what we are looking for will make sure the path is not lost and stay the course when the going gets rough.

I would like to thank you for taking this leg of your journey with me, and I hope you never stop reaching for your highest light.

Crisis

Should you find yourself in dire straits, suicidal thoughts, or violent impulses, and none of this is helping- please do not give in. Reach out and seek help. There are hotlines for all the major crises and catch-alls for the obscure. I mentioned it above, but I'll shout it here near the end: *seeking help is not a sign of weakness but strength*. Acknowledging you have reached the limit of what you can handle, take the extra step and seek a professional. Mistrust and being poor are not the obstacles you think they are. There is help available and within reach.

CPSIA information can be obtained
at www.ICGtesting.com
Printed in the USA
BVHW070218240122
627003BV00005B/138